# GROWING VINES TO MAKE WINES

## Nick Poulter

An Amateur Winemaker Book

Special Interest Model Books Ltd.
P.O.Box 327
Poole
Dorset
BH15 2RG
England

First published by Nexus Special Interests Ltd. 1998
This edition published by Special Interest Model Books Ltd. 2005

ISBN 1-85486-181-6

Printed and bound in Great Britain by Biddles Ltd. www.biddles.co.uk

# ᘓ Contents

# ଔ Introduction

Twenty-five years ago, in my first book *Growing Vines*, I wrote "The British have been so indoctrinated with the fallacy that they do not have the climate for outdoor grapegrowing that it is hard to persuade them otherwise by argument alone". Today, however, there are few who do not know of the still growing number of commercial vineyards in the countryside or of the many amateurs cropping vines in their gardens.

This book is intended primarily as an aid to these amateurs and it is hoped that those readers who do not already grow their own outdoor grapes will be encouraged to join the thousands who do. Grape-growing, for both winemaking and dessert use, is one of the most rewarding and satisfying pastimes there is and it must be regretted that there is so little written on the subject in English. With isolated exceptions, most of southern England and Wales is suitable for unprotected garden grapes and indeed early varieties will flourish a long way north on a good site. In all but the cooler areas there is no need to have a sunny wall or similar protection; after all, the English commercial vineyards are in open fields.

All that the grower has to do is plant suitable varieties and follow certain simple rules. Grapes that are not properly ripe will never produce good wine, no matter how much sugaring is done, and some varieties will never ripen here. This should come as no surprise – the Germans, for instance, obviously do not plant the same varieties as the Spanish. There are several vine varieties which are well suited to *our* conditions, and their culture, as I shall explain, is well within anyone's capabilities.

Whether your wine production is one gallon or fifty, the principles of vinting are the same, and the size of your vintage should have very little to do with the quality of your product. If you are able to make a barrel of wine you may count yourself lucky, but if you have room to grow only a few bottles your wine can be every bit as fine. Whatever your output, excellence should be your aim, and excellence can only be achieved by growing suitable vine varieties in the right manner, and by carrying out careful vinification. The best English wine is very good indeed, and the amateur is quite capable of achieving the highest standard provided the trouble is taken to do so.

Only two considerations limit your wine production. First, unless you wish to give a lot of wine away or 'go commercial', there is no point in growing more wine than you or your family can drink. However, a more practical limit as far as most people are concerned is the availability of the planting area. Fortunately quite a good crop can be obtained from a very small area, and even the tiniest garden can grow one or two gallons of wine.

At the other end of the scale, a hogshead might be thought by most people to be quite beyond their reach, and it must be admitted that many simply do not have room for this size of production. However, the area required to grow a hogshead of wine is less than one-tenth of an acre or the approximate equivalent of a plot measuring 20 × 24 yards (18 × 22 metres). This will contain about two hundred vines. Perhaps it is appropriate that as we are members of the European Community, Britons should adopt the widespread and agreeable custom of the family wine-patch. Indeed many are already planting on this scale, and with the prospect of fine quality wine at a material cost of a few pounds a year who can blame them?

I should emphasise that the methods and procedures given here are for the treatment of *freshly gathered wine grapes*. Of course, those who wish to, may use the same techniques to assist them in making wine from dessert grapes purchased commercially, but they should not expect to make such inexpensive wine and they certainly will not achieve the same quality. Naturally, grapes for wine production and those for dessert use are not only cultivated differently, but more often than not come from quite different varieties. The dessert grape will yield only ordinary wine as its composition is balanced for eating. Some of the elements essential for high quality wine will either be missing or inadequate. However, contrary to popular belief, many wine varieties can be made to produce excellent eating fruit.

At first glance some of the methods described in the following pages may appear frighteningly scientific to the beginner, but one reading should convince even the most timid that they are really within the capability of all. Anyone who can learn to read a hydrometer – and I have yet to meet the person who cannot – will be able to master all the techniques mentioned in this book. I have endeavoured to explain every step fully using plain language, and where I mention equipment that is not within the easy reach of everyone I give alternatives. If you are a keen country winemaker, some, though maybe not all, of the methods described will be familiar to you. However, I have tried to make the text complete but concise and practical for the novice.

Although now retired after twenty-five years as a partner in an English commercial vineyard, I began grape-growing with a few vines in my garden in the Thames Valley. As a result of my early difficulties in obtaining guidance on the subject, I have tried to put into this book all that I would have liked to have known when I started myself.

There is a world of difference between growing a small plot of vines for family wine and investing £100,000 in a commercial vineyard and winery, and those who wish to grow commercially will have to acquire greater knowledge than it is the intention of this book to give. The main aim of this book is to encourage the culture of outdoor vines, but I include a chapter for the increasing number of gardeners whose interest also lies in the greenhouse.

A list of suppliers of vines, materials and equipment plus a bibliography for further reading can be found in the Appendices.

# ₢ 1 The history of vine-growing in England

Much of the early disbelief in the possibility of an English viticultural revival stemmed from some rather quaint ideas of the history of grape-growing in this country. It is not commonly understood that the former decline of wine-growing in England was the result of not one but several factors. Although shrouded in the mists of time, there is a surprising wealth of records of viticulture – enough to show us what happened. Very briefly the story is as follows ....

We know from the vessels found in his graves, that British Iron Age man drank wine, but at this early date it is most likely that all the wine drunk in Britain had in fact been grown further south, and was imported here in the course of trade. By the time the Romans had occupied the country the vine had made its appearance, and it seems that it is they who introduced the plant. It was one of the many gifts Britannia received from Rome. When the Romans eventually left these shores, their successors continued to culture the vine, and in the Saxon period many references were made in manuscripts, such as Bede, and in the laws and accounts of the kings and landowners. One chronicler of the time said of the Isle of Ely that "it is so thickly planted with apples and vines that it is an earthly paradise", and in fact the area became known as the Isle of Vines.

The first comprehensive list of vineyards appeared after the Norman conquest, in the *Domesday Book*. This great work of 1088 detailed some thirty-eight vineyards in England, giving their size and sometimes their output. These vineyards were often extensive, one at Belcamp in Essex owned by Ralph Baignard, for example, being eighteen arpents or about twenty-three acres (9.5ha) in extent. The future of English viticulture at this period seemed assured and then in 1152 Henry II married Eleanor of Acquitaine and the first blow fell. Part of Eleanor's dowry was the Garonne district of France and with it the prolific wine-producing area near Bordeaux. Suddenly it was possible to import large quantities of cheap wine. It is likely that the quality of English wine was little if at all inferior, but it was much more expensive to grow. The English land-owners reasoned that it was better to import cheap southern wine and put their own vineyards to a more profitable use. Land suitable for arable use was scarce, and wheat and barley were always in need. The vineyards did not completely disappear overnight but they began to dwindle. Some were ploughed up and fewer were planted.

Then, in the middle of the fourteenth century, there was a small but significant climatic change and the summers became less favourable. Some vineyards still continued but their profitability was less certain. By the sixteenth century most of the remaining vineyards were in the hands of the ecclesiastical orders and with the dissolution of the monasteries by Henry VIII between 1536 and 1539, vineyards as a regu-lar feature of the countryside ceased to exist.

From that time on viticultural ventures were infrequent and isolated. Vineyards such as that owned by Colonel Blount in the time of Charles II at Blackheath appeared from time to time but they were no longer com-mon. Towards the end of the eighteenth century a vineyard of some re-pute was planted by Charles Hamilton at Painshill in Surrey. The vines were of two varieties: the *Auvernat*, a grape from Burgundy and the Loire, and the *Pinot Meunier* of the Champagne. At first vintage red wine was made but it proved to be harsh, after that only white was made. The grapes were picked as late as the season allowed and care was taken to prevent premature fermentation taking place by transporting the grapes from the vineyard in small containers, thus avoiding self-pressing. Fermentation was carried out in hogsheads and judging by contempo-rary accounts it was usually fairly violent. Obviously quality was taken seriously as only the juice from the first two pressings was used.

After fermentation the wine was racked off into clean hogsheads, and in March a fining was carried out by means of the application of fish glue. Soon afterwards the wine was bottled and it was said to be fit to drink as soon as six weeks later. It was not a long-keeping wine and it was best drunk before it was more than a year old, denoting that sulphuring was probably not done. The quality was generally agreed to be excellent and the selling price of 7/6d to 10/6d per bottle at that time speaks for itself. At one sale alone £500 worth was sold to a single London wine merchant at a rate of fifty guineas a hogshead. But it seems that even in an age of eccentrics Charles Hamilton was considered eccentric and when he died his vineyard seems to have died with him. Either he left no heirs or they were incompetent vintners.

A hundred years later the last of the historic wine-growing ventures was started by another eccentric, the Marquis of Bute. In 1875 he planted five acres of vines at Castell Coch, north of Cardiff. After a few trials he decided on the *Gamay Noir*. Several poor years in a row as the vines were coming into bearing did not help and success did not come easily. However, the Marquis was both wealthy and determined, and another five acres were planted in 1886 at Swanbridge in the Vale of Glamorgan. A temporary planting was also made at St Quentins near Lowbridge, but it seems that neither wealth nor determination made for true success and in the forty years of the vineyard's existence only seven vintages were reported to be good. In 1916 the vineyards were ploughed up to produce food for the war effort and they were never replanted.

Had a more suitable variety been selected, success might well have been achieved. It had obviously become accepted at this stage that the vine was unable to flourish this far north and it was plainly heretical to question this dogma. Those few who tried to grow vines usually grew totally unsuited varieties and used incorrect pruning methods, and their failures merely reinforced the fallacy that the vine was a tender and difficult plant, with no place in England.

Fortunately during the first half of the twentieth century much happened in the viticultural world. Many new varieties were produced in continental research stations, and a good deal was discovered about the metabolism of the vine and what the plant required in the way of conditions and treatment. In the 1950s a few pioneers realised this and some considered it worthwhile trying once again to re-establish the vine in England. Many trials had to be carried out and much had to be learned by experience. It was found, for example, that a variety did not always behave in the way it might have been expected to. Some very promising varieties failed while others which had seemed less promising thrived, but it soon became evident that certain varieties in certain localities would not only ripen their fruit but could produce excellent wine. The old myth was shattered at last.

In 1966 there were only seven acres (3ha) of commercial vineyards in the whole of England, but further planting took place at an accelerating rate. By 1996 the area had risen to 965 ha (2,400 acres). In an average year this will yield nine million bottles. Most vineyards are of a modest 4 or 5 acres (2ha), but a few are as much as 30 acres (12.5ha). Quality varies from fairly ordinary to superb, with an increasing number raising their standards ever higher. Some English wine is competing with, and surpassing, wines from the continent and other parts of the world. In spite of this, the industry has not received much help or encouragement from the government when one considers that the annual duty and VAT collected is around £400 per acre.

A line from an old Burgundian song still sung at the wine sales festivities held at Beaune runs: "May the English never have the vine, the pretty vine". But now the English have it, and with care they intend to keep it.

# ᚼ 2 The English climate

It has already been implied that we tend to have a national inferiority complex about our climate, but how many have really taken the trouble to compare it to that of the northerly continental vine-growing regions? The answer is very few, for those who have done so will have realised that much of our country compares very favourably. We often hear such comments as "It rains all summer here", and yet the fact is that most of the country suffers an agricultural drought more than five summers in every ten. Others say "We don't get enough sun", and yet a few areas in England get more than almost the entire German vine-growing region and many more receive equal amounts. As for frosts, we have less dangerous late spring frosts than they do on the continent and our less severe winter frosts present no dangers at all.

The vine is not the tender difficult plant some would have us believe. It is tough, very hardy in winter and amazingly adaptable. The most important climatic factors as far as the vine is concerned are those of rainfall, sunshine hours and air temperature. Taking rainfall first, there is no part of the country too dry for mature vines although young vines in dry spells require watering just as any other plants do. A very few areas, generally confined to high places, do have excessive rainfall, but as they are usually mountainous or moorland they are inclined to be too elevated and cool anyway. Our June/July period, which is the flowering period, is usually drier than the same period on the Mosel and this helps our vines to set good crops of fruit.

As for sunshine hours, different varieties require different amounts, and most of the varieties which thrive in this country are affected less by direct sunlight than by temperature. Those who think that vines require sunlight all through the day are mistaken. It may be an advantage, but it is not as important as people often believe. Many varieties do well when they get direct sunlight for a maximum of only three hours in any day, so if you have a garden which loses the sun for much of the day do not be discouraged.

When it comes to temperature, there is a difference between the season we expect here and that normally experienced in Germany. This difference is not so much in the *amount* of heat we receive as in the timing. For example, in the hottest months of July and August the average temperature on the Mosel may be one degree higher than the temperature, shall we say, on the Thames, but in September and October, the very important ripening months, the average temperature on the Thames is often *more* than one degree higher than that on the Mosel. This tendency is due to our oceanic climate with its more temperate but longer growing season. Gardens, in fact, have some advantages over the larger commercial vineyards, for while the garden is usually sheltered by houses, trees and fences the large vineyard is

Table 1   Comparison of English and continental climatic data (30 year average), April to October.

| Locality | Rainfall total (mm) | Sunshine hours | Heat total (degree-days over 8°C) |
|---|---|---|---|
| ENGLAND | | | |
| Cambridge | 319 | 1182 | 1142 |
| Cheltenham | 399 | 1142 | 1163 |
| Kew | 359 | 1147 | 1262 |
| Norwich | 399 | 1229 | 1129 |
| Plymouth | 484 | 1272 | 1129 |
| Sandown | 388 | 1385 | 1326 |
| Tunbridge Wells | 408 | 1268 | 1102 |
| GERMANY | | | |
| Ahrweiler (Ahr) | 401 | 1061 | 1204 |
| Bernkastel (Mosel) | 443 | 1193 | 1326 |
| Trier (Mosel) | 443 | 1259 | 1378 |
| FRANCE | | | |
| Rheims (Champagne) | 369 | 1312 | 1369 |

exposed to the wind. As a result the air temperature in the average garden will often rise far above that experienced in a large vineyard.

Table 1 makes comparisons between sites in this country and some in northern continental vine-growing regions. It can be seen that we compare not unfavourably.

## Frost precautions

The vine is no more susceptible to frost damage than the apple, except that the apple usually bears its blossom higher off the ground. The only time of year when the vine is vulnerable to frost is in the spring, at or after bud-burst. As this is not until late April or May damage is uncommon except in bad frost hollows. If dwarf apple trees are often damaged by frost in your area, you may have difficulty with your vines, but covering the canes with newspaper when frosty nights are forecast will usually provide a simple and effective protection. When frosts nip the first buds, replacement shoots are soon grown.

# ❧ 3 Vine varieties

The choice of the correct variety of vine is of the greatest importance. Many people think of the vine as if it were just one variety and believe that they all require the same climate. This is very far from the truth, for some varieties will thrive where others will fail miserably. The variety Black Hamburg, for example, is grown in the open vineyard in Alsace, but in England, except in very hot summers, it is suited only to the cold-house. Yet we often hear of those persevering with this variety outdoors, and only getting a ripe crop once or twice in ten years.

There are more than thirty varieties which will grow well and ripen their crops in England, but some are so much better than others that it is not worth cultivating more than a few. New vine varieties are produced only by crossing two other varieties, and the chance of producing a new vine which is even as good as its parents is about one in ten thousand. It can be seen therefore that vine breeding is not an easy task and growing vines from pips is generally a complete waste of time.

Before rushing into planting vines, you should give careful thought as to what type of wine you wish to produce, and perhaps more important, the type of wine it is practicable to grow in your area.

Different viticultural zones best produce different types of wine, and you are not always lucky enough to be born in the region where your favourite wines come from. We are a northerly wine-growing region and it is sensible to look at the continental viticultural areas which most closely resemble our own. These are the Lower Rhine, Mosel and Ahr rivers of Germany and possibly the Champagne of France. Undoubtedly the greatest proportion of wine from these areas is white, though some light red wine is also grown. Sparkling wine comes from the Champagne and Germany, and from the latter country comes also the fabulous dessert Auslese-type wines. These cool-region wines are those we are most likely to succeed with here, and we will look briefly at each type and consider its merits.

The European vine, although existing as many different varieties, is really only one species, *Vitis vinifera sativa.* In the USA this did not exist before it was introduced there by man, but there are several other species which are native to the USA such as *Vitis riparia, Vitis labrusca, Vitis berlandieri,* etc. The American species produce juice which is greatly inferior to that of the European vine. They do tend to be more vigorous, however, and for this reason and in the effort to produce more disease-resistant varieties, attempts were made to cross the European and American vines to produce offspring with European quality and American heavy cropping.

In viticulture the term 'hybrid' is applied only to those varieties which owe some of their ancestry to one of the American or Caucasian species. The first hybrids in the nineteenth century produced not only American vine vigour, but also the comparatively poor juice quality. More recently however, hybrids have been produced which not only produce prolific crops but also have good quality juice of European character. Typical of these are Seyval Blanc and Triomphe d'Alsace.

Many of the varieties we grow in Europe are crosses between pure-bred European varieties such as Siegerrebe whose parents are Madeleine Angevine and Gewurztraminer. The offspring of pure European parents are called 'crosses', not hybrids.

White grapes can, of course, only produce white wine, but red grapes can produce red, white or rosé depending on whether the grapes are pressed straight away or put into the fermenting vats for a certain time. In northerly latitudes some of the red varieties actually produce a better white or pink wine than they do red. All the finest wine in northern regions is white, though this is not to say that good red wine cannot be grown. In recent years some really very good red wine has been produced, although this has usually been in some of the exceptionally hot summers we have had in the last ten years. If you have a particularly good microclimate, by all means try growing some red wine, but only white is likely to yield the best quality every year.

People often ask what variety they should grow to produce a sweet or a dry wine. The answer to this one is that any variety can make either a sweet or a dry wine depending on what the vintner wants. Commercially speaking, with the exception of some special wines such as Auslese, all wines are fermented dry and then sweetened to suit the market.

As so often happens in nature, fruit growing near the limits of its climatic range is unequalled in quality and English grapes are no exception. English wine can be of an unsurpassed excellence.

The varieties listed below are not the only varieties which will grow here but they include the best available to the amateur. Some excellent varieties have been produced by some of the continental breeding stations but unfortunately they are seldom available for amateur planting. This is due to the fact that for some years newly bred varieties such as Reichensteiner, Faber, Bacchus and Wurzer have been registered for Breeder's Rights. This means that only licenced nurserymen may propagate these varieties, and a small royalty must be paid by those nurserymen to the viticultural institute that produced the variety. This is quite fair when you consider the effort required to breed a succcessful new variety but it means that few nurserymen in this country, if any, propagate these plants. On the other hand, there are those who import them from the continent for growers here.

The ripening period of grapes varies according to variety, site and weather. Outdoor vines will ripen their crop between mid-September and early November, though most are ready to pick in mid-October. It is not possible to lay down hard and fast rules but in descriptions given here it may be taken that 'early' means ripening before the end of September in most years. Mid-season grapes ripen during the first three weeks of October, and late varieties after that. Of course dates vary a little from year to year, but very wide differences from the norm are rare.

## Sparkling wines

Theoretically at least we have good climatic conditions in England for sparkling wine production, and it may be asked why, at the time of writing, few commercial vineyards here make this product. I know of only one or two vineyards which make a sparkling wine, but it is largely a matter of economics.

The production of sparkling wine is rather more complicated than that of still table wine. More labour and equipment is required, and a higher price must be obtained for the product to justify the extra vinification costs. Low-price sparkling wine only becomes economic when great quantities are made by means of the tank or carbonation processes, from comparatively low-priced fruit, as in some of the German Sekt production. Therefore although it may well be possible for the commercial English grower to make the equivalent of good Champagne, it is only now being tried on a small scale. The amateur, however, may walk where the professional fears to tread!

Although any grape juice can be turned into sparkling wine, it is wise to select a variety which has adequate natural juice acid. Wrotham Pinot suggests itself as an obvious candidate because its continental sister is used in champagne production. Another variety which should perform well is Seyval Blanc.

I have already mentioned the extra time and equipment necessary for this type of wine, and the process is described briefly in Chapter 16, but I should also mention at this stage that more skill is required too. Unless obsessed with the idea, it would probably be wise to approach sparkling winemaking as a development of table wine production so that should the techniques prove too difficult to master, you are able to revert to still wine in later vintages without replanting some of your vines.

## Dessert wines

Expressing a purely personal opinion, I am bound to say that I consider the luscious Auslese-type wines of Germany as being the peak of perfection of northern wines. Not that I would want to drink them exclusively for the rest of my life! These wines are usually naturally sweet, but have such a full and exquisite bouquet and flavour that many who normally prefer dry wines cannot help relishing them.

Like sparkling wines, they are more difficult to produce than table wines, but whereas the former is more difficult mainly in the vinting, dessert wines are more difficult in the growing.

It is not at all easy to describe the honey-like qualities of these special wines and only tasting will really suffice. The experience is well worth the cost, however, although a bottle will set you back £10 or even a little more. The cost of these wines is due partly to the extra skill in growing, harvesting and vinting and partly to the fact that grapes used to produce dessert wines yield only about half the normal quantity of juice. Those who wish to experience the delights of these wines before attempting to produce their like should try the Auslese wines of Germany, or the best Sauternes like Chateau Guiraud, or Barsac such as Chateau Climens. The latter wines should not be confused with the ordinaires of these districts which are as different as chalk and cheese.

Before you can even consider making a dessert wine, your crop must reach a certain degree of ripeness and for this reason only those living in the warmer counties should contemplate attempting it. As already stated, most amateurs are in a better position than commercial growers as far as microclimate is concerned due to the fact that gardens are generally far more sheltered than our open vineyards. This in turn means a higher thermal build-up around the amateur's vines with correspondingly higher juice gravities. Obviously this is to the advantage of the garden grower when it comes to dessert wine production.

In order to elevate the juice sugar even more and at the same time impart a very special and distinctive flavour, we let nature help us. Infection of the ripening berries by the mould *Botrytis cinerea* is not only desirable but essential. *Botrytis* spores are to be found around us everywhere floating in the air, and precautions must be taken to prevent it attacking the vine's crop before a certain stage of ripeness. However, once this stage is reached infection is not undesirable, even in a table wine crop, and it must be positively *encouraged* in a dessert wine crop.

Briefly, the reason why it is so beneficial in these circumstances is that the mildew extracts more water from the grape than it does sugar, mainly by allowing evaporation. By this natural process the juice of the berry is concentrated, thus elevating the gravity. At the same time glycerine and other compounds are produced and the acidity is reduced.

The crop gravity to aim for is about 120°Oe. In open vineyard conditions this is not easily achieved although late pickings in English vineyards have approached this value. The vintage for these wines may be delayed into December or even into the New Year! One method of accelerating ripening and encouraging *botrytis* is that of covering the lower fruiting portion of the vine with polythene sheet. This technique is sometimes used in Germany and is illustrated in Fig. 1. Not only do the grapes benefit from the greenhouse effect of the polythene, but the comparative lack of ventilation promotes those conditions which favour mould development, while protecting the infected berries from being 'washed out' by rain. *Botrytis* is unable to penetrate the grape skin unaided but usually the skin will be thin enough late in the season, and

**Figure 1**   *The use of polythene to encourage botrytis.*

have enough tiny lacerations due to such agencies as weather damage to allow entry of mould spores. The polythene should not be attached to the vines until the beginning of September or other undesirable mildews such as peronospera and oidium will also be encouraged, and far from aiding you they will ruin the crop.

Even if you intend to make a table wine and your fruit develops *botrytis* late in the season, please do not discard it! As long as the fruit is moist inside the quality of the juice will, if anything, be improved although the bunch may appear disgusting. On the other hand, if the mould is so advanced that it has sucked the berries quite dry, these must be cut out or their inclusion will impart a musty flavour to the wine.

Conversely, if you are attempting a dessert wine and *botrytis* infection fails, all is not lost. Simply make a table wine instead.

## Blending juices

Many famous wines are made from one grape only. Chambertin for example is made from the Pinot Noir, Hungarian Bull's Blood from the Kadarka and Sercial Madeira from the grape of that name. Other renowned wines are made from a blend of two or more grapes – Chateau Haut-Brion is made from Cabernet Sauvignon, Cabernet Franc and Merlot grapes while Chateau d'Yquem comes from the Semillon and the Sauvignon Blanc.

These blends are made because each grape gives something to the wine which enhances it and improves the balance. Garden growers should follow this example rather than mixing the juice of all their varieties simply because they have them growing. For this reason it is sensible to have as many vines of as few varieties as possible. The grower who has room for only four plants would be much wiser to plant all Mueller-Thurgau, or two Mueller-Thurgau and two Seyve Villard, rather than four different varieties. Too many varieties used in the production of one wine often produces a mixture of perfumes and flavours which confuse the senses and the total effect is spoiled. Some blends are excellent but tend to err on the side of simplicity.

## Outdoor white varieties

In character northern white wines are fresh and flowery, though they may be full and rich too. Their bouquet is often superb and they retain a grapiness that few other wines can match. The perfume on opening a bottle should give you the same pleasure as a breath of spring air in a blossoming orchard. To this end great care must be taken in the vinification to prevent loss of freshness. The best juice can be ruined by slap-happy vinting.

These wines often possess a faint but pleasant sparkle. The Germans term this *spritzig* meaning prickling or lively, and enjoyment of the wine is undoubtedly enhanced by its presence. Regrettably the characteristic is harder to achieve when making only a couple of gallons as it is due to absorbed carbon dioxide which is less easily retained in a small quantity.

White wine is usually made from white grapes as you might expect, but it is not in the least difficult to make it from black grapes also. Only hybrid black grape varieties which owe some of their parentage to one of the American species have coloured juice. In European varieties the colour is all in the skin and it can be left behind by pressing the fruit straight after picking. This technique is perfectly illustrated by champagne which is largely produced from black grape varieties.

## *Mueller-Thurgau*

The most famous grape of Germany is the Riesling and it is in that country that it excels as it does nowhere else. In Yugoslavia, with its hotter summer, Riesling makes good enough wine but it is seldom exciting, whereas on the Rhine and Mosel it can be superb. Unfortunately this vine is rather late in England, seeming to require higher peak summer temperatures than we can regularly count on. However, luckily an offspring of this vine does exceptionally well here. This offspring is called Mueller-Thurgau although it is popularly known in England as Riesling Sylvaner. In fact it is believed to be a Riesling x Riesling cross.

This vine is very widely planted in Germany, accounting for nearly a quarter of all vines planted, though it does not reach the Riesling standard there. But just as Riesling excels in Germany so Mueller-Thurgau excels here and is capable of producing a wine superior to that made from the same grape on the continent. This is almost certainly due to climatic differences. Although some regions here receive about the same summer heat income as locations on the Mosel, our summer has slightly less of a temperature peak at the hottest time of the year, but makes up for it by extending later into the autumn. This longer gentler season appears to bring out the best in Mueller-Thurgau.

*1. Mueller-Thurgau.*

The variety is undoubtedly the most thoroughly proven in this country and is, in my opinion, the most outstanding wine grape available to the amateur.

Pruned in the normal way, to about four feet of cane per plant, Mueller-Thurgau should yield around two bottles of wine per stock. Being a variety which is naturally low in acidity it is not well suited to very late picking. The optimum juice gravity is in the region of 70°–75° Oechles. If allowed to rise much above this value the acid level will fall to the point where the resulting wine lacks life.

The Oechles scale, measured in °Oe, is of German origin but has been adopted here. It is very simple, merely using the numerals after the decimal point in the specific gravity of a juice or must. Hence a specific gravity of 1.070 = 70°Oe and 1.124 = 124°Oe. Specific gravities are discussed in greater detail in Chapter 11 under the description of the use of the hydrometer.

### Seyval Blanc (Seyve Villard 5276)

Another excellent source of white juice is the vine Seyve Blanc. Wine from this variety on its own can be excellent, but often it tends to be rather neutral in character. However, blended with juice from

*2. Seyval Blanc.*

Mueller-Thurgau it performs beautifully. The ratio of the blend need not be exact, but by growing an equal number of both vines the resulting blend will perfectly suit most people's taste. Seyve Blanc is generally more prolific than Mueller-Thurgau, producing around three bottles per plant. A mixture of these varieties therefore results in both quantity and quality, and growers with limited space will find the arrangement ideal. The acidity of Seyve Blanc is adequate and there is no upper limit to the desirable juice gravity.

## *Madeleine Angevine 7972*

A heavy cropper of very good flavour for both eating and winemaking. This is a very early variety and therefore especially suitable for those living in a cool area. It is a highly reliable cropper even in the most unfavourable years.

*3. Madeleine Angevine 7972.*

## *Madeleine Sylvaner 2851*

Probably the earliest of all varieties to ripen in this country. Another fine dual purpose grape ideal for less favoured sites.

*4. Madeleine Sylvaner 2851.*

## *Siegerrebe*

A lovely early ripening grape with a pronounced Muscat flavour. Fully ripe the grapes change from translucent green through gold to rosy amber. It benefits from shelter to assist good pollination.

## *Chardonnay*

A comparatively late season ripener which seems to do best in inland areas where peak temperatures are generally higher than those on the coast. It is really only suited to winemaking, yielding a product with a good Chablis character.

*5. Siegerrebe.*

*6. Pinot Blanc.*

## Pinot Blanc

Similar in general appearance to Chardonnay, in my experience a superior variety in both yield and quality in this country. Late season, but even in the awful summer of 1980 it gave us fine wine in considerable quantity. Not widely planted in England at the time of writing but I am sure it soon will be.

## Gewurztraminer

A selected strain of Traminer famous for the spicy wines of Alsace. It is similar in character to Siegerrebe but later ripening.

## Himrod

A seedless grape of good quality for both dessert use and wine, which ripens mid-season.

*7. Himrod.*

## Black outdoor varieties

The vinting of red wine differs from white at an early stage, but the extra equipment required is minimal and need be no deterrent to the vintner. However, although you may hope to compete very favourably with a good Rhine, Mosel or Alsatian white wine, we do not normally get the heat to produce the finest reds. Twenty years ago very few, if any, English vineyards produced red wine but the recent trend towards more exceptional summers has led some to venture into this field with surprisingly good results.

The amateur usually has the advantage of a small, sheltered plot where temperatures build up to higher levels than they do on breezy hillsides, so provided you do not live too far north by all means try your hand at red wine.

### *Wrotham Pinot*

An interesting variety springing from stock found growing in Kent in the 1940s. It is in fact a strain of Pinot Meunier used for champagne production. We never found this ripened sufficiently consistently at our vineyard on the Isle of Wight. Contrary to popular belief, summer temperatures on the south coast are generally lower than those inland farther north. For this reason we often heard of inland growers getting good results from this variety when ours were indifferent.

### *Seibel 13053*

For many years the best grape for the production of red wine in this country. Cropping is very heavy, ripening is early or mid-season and the wine is fruity with a good colour. This variety used to have a dubious reputation due to some fallacious rumours. After faulty experimentation carried out many years ago it was believed that the substance Malvidin 3.5 diglucoside found in certain grapes, including Seibel, was responsible for liver damage (in chickens). This work has since been totally discredited and you may safely drink the wine from Seibel grapes without any worry of toxicity.

*8. Seibel 13053.*

## *Triomphe d'Alsace*

Without doubt the best red wine variety available to the amateur and responsible for some very drinkable commercial English reds. A fairly vigorous vine but with easily controlled productive growth which is comparatively disease-resistant.

## *Pirovano 14*

Well suited to the cooler parts of the country due to its early ripening. It is a grape that also makes a good eater owing to its large berries and good flavour.

*9. Triomphe d'Alsace.*
*10. Pirovano 14.*

*1. Mueller-Thurgau.*

*2. Seyval Blanc.*

*3. Madeleine Angevine 7972.*

4. *Madeleine Sylvaner 2851.*

5. *Siegerrebe.*

6. *Pinot Blanc.*

7. *Himrod.*

*8. Seibel 13053.*

*9. Triomphe d'Alsace.*

*10. Pirovano 14.*

*11. Gagarin Blue.*

12. Brant.

13. Strawberry Grape.

14. Baco.

*11. Gagarin Blue.*

## Gagarin Blue

Like Pirovano, this variety owes some of its ancestry to the Asian vine species *Vitis amurensis*. The oval blue-black berries are large and are held in heavy bunches. They make excellent eating, but they also make very good wine. Ripening is early to mid-season.

## Tereshkova

Another *amurensis* cross which is similar in character to Gagarin Blue but rather more vigorous in growth with rounder berries. Also, like Gagarin Blue, it breaks bud comparatively late in spring, making it a good choice for frost pocket areas.

## Leon Millot

A prolific producer of very early ripening fruit in the form of small, tight bunches which nevertheless make excellent wine.

## *Marshall Joffre*

In most respects very similar to Leon Millot but an even earlier ripener.

## Outdoor vines of interest

### *Brant (or Brandt)*

Not particularly recommended for wine, which is never better than ordinary, but worth mentioning because it is so well known for its autumn leaf colour in a 'colouring' year. By all means grow it, but for its decorative effect rather than its quality.

### *Strawberry Grape*

An unusual, vigorous vine with large matt leaves, and fruit with a flavour a little like that of strawberries which some love and others detest. This flavour is due to its American parentage and can be an acquired taste. That said, there are those who greatly appreciate it.

*12. Brant.*

13. *Strawberry Grape.*

14. *Baco.*

## *Baco*

A very vigorous variety requiring lots of room. Not really recommended for either wine or dessert use in this country as it needs heat to bring out any quality. However, for rapid decorative growth it cannot be surpassed. At its peak, shoot growth can exceed 30cm a day.

# ❧ 4 The site, soil and spacing

The commercial grower this far north will, if possible, find a southerly slope, though some use level ground and at least one large vineyard in Kent is planted on slopes which are mainly northerly in aspect. This is not the disadvantage it might at first seem because of the good shelter offered from the prevailing, cooling south-west winds during the summer.

As mentioned before, the amateur in a garden will often have a more favourable microclimate than that found in the open vineyards, so do not think it is necessary to have a veritable suntrap. Those who have fences and walls in their garden will find it convenient to use them for vines, but vines on trellises in the open are more usual and of course this is the only way in which they will be found in large vineyards. If you do use walls, although a south-facing wall is best, there is nothing to stop you using a wall which faces east or west. Experience has shown that vines which get direct sunlight for no more than three hours in a day still flourish in most areas.

The soil is naturally important to any plant but the vine is tolerant of a very wide range of types. Reasonable drainage is desirable but the vine will thrive in the heaviest clay as long as surface water can run off in the winter.

If the soil is sandy or particularly light it is, of course, important to fertilize it more often than other soils as the nutrients will be leached out more easily. Do not believe the old wives' tale 'the poorer the soil, the better the wine', although it might be true to say that the vine will flourish in soil that will grow little else. Certainly if a soil is too rich it is likely to produce verdant growth with a much reduced fruit yield.

While clays may sometimes present drainage problems and can be cold and heavy to work, they are usually very fertile. If your soil is sodden for most of the year, including the summer, it must be drained. In particularly difficult sites where proper drainage is not possible, vines may be planted in substantial mounds or ridges which provide a good volume of free-draining soil. Our vineyard was on very heavy clay, being extremely sticky in the winter and like concrete in summer if not tilled, but our vines flourished and bore lovely crops.

If you have a *very* chalky soil and your vines make slow growth, you can do much to modify the soil around the vines by digging in humus and manure (not mushroom compost, which is usually lime-laden), and by using acid-reaction fertilizers. In very difficult cases, vines that have been grafted on to 41B rootstock should be grown.

A vine is like any other plant and if not fed it will produce poorer crops each year and may eventually stop bearing altogether. Even when a soil is fairly well supplied with nutrients, the vine will remove some of these each season with the crop, leaves and canes, and what is removed must be replaced one way or another. Farmyard manure or compost is very valuable, not so much for the food it contains, which is very little, but mainly because it helps to keep the soil biologically active. Plants need carbon dioxide during the day in order that they may carry out photosynthesis, and the soil bacteria supply much of this by breaking down organic matter. In addition to organic matter, the vine needs mineral salts which are most conveniently added in the form of fertilizer compounds. No soil is exactly the same as any other but, assuming that your soil is in reasonable balance the table on page 32 will give you a fertilizer programme that should suit your vines. In addition, if the soil is deficient in lime it is a good idea to turn in chalk at a rate of 120g per sq metre (4oz/sq yd) every two or three years. The ideal soil pH is around 6.5. Do not add chalk if the pH is higher.

Your vines are really the best indicator of how well balanced your soil is. Meagre growth and pale leaves are usually a sign of nitrogen deficiency. If the vine takes on a really yellow appearance in the summer it is probably suffering from chlorosis which is due to an excess of lime in the soil, causing an imbalance which renders it difficult for the plant to take up iron. This may be overcome by the use of chelated iron compounds such as *Sequestrine*. On the other hand, the appearance of leaves which remain green close to the veins but turn yellow between them is a classic sign of magnesium deficiency (see photograph). This may be dealt with quite simply with a soil dressing of magnesium sulphate (Epsom Salts). Try an application of 120g/sq m (4oz/sq yd). After watering in if necessary in drought conditions, allow a month to see if new leaf growth returns to normal before being tempted to apply any more. Older leaves showing a bluish discolouration on the upper surface indicate a lack of phosphorous. Leaves dying or browning from the edges inwards may indicate potassium deficiency, but if you have suffered bad gales it might also just be wind burn.

There are several other elements that the vine requires for health but most of them are required in small quantities and few soils are badly lacking in these trace elements. If you suspect or have it confirmed that your soil is deficient in these substances there are several compound fertilizers readily available to the gardener which will rectify the situation.

The fertilizer programme below is for mature vines. Young vines in their first two years of life need only half the quantity of fertilizers recommended.

Within reason herbaceous plants may be grown right up to vines as long as they do not shade or crowd them. In this way it is possible to

*15. Typical leaf symptoms of magnesium deficiency.*

grow vines at the back of normal flower borders. However, in the first two years of a vine's life give it as little competition as possible.

It is most important that any *summer* application of nitrogen is delayed until after the flower has set its fruit, or it will cause poor fruit set. Summer nitrogen is only necessary if growth is weak. Over-vigorous growth is nothing but trouble.

## Soil cultivation

To prevent compaction of the surface due to walking around the vines, and to control weeds, simple cultivation should be carried out from time to time. Fertilizers should also be hoed in. Do not dig too deeply around vines for some of the roots run within a few inches of the surface. These 'day-roots' are of great importance in taking up nutrients and although they will grow again if damaged, their temporary loss can be harmful at certain times of the year. Having said this, in our vineyard, which was on heavy clay, we ridged the soil up along the vine rows and ceased tilling the soil altogether. Compaction did not seem to be a problem although the surface became firm for feet and tractor, and we were spared the annoyance of slopping around in deep mud after rain. Weed control was entirely by rapidly degradable herbicides, of which more later.

**Fertilizer programme for mature grapevines.**

| Time of application | Fertilizer | Application rates[*] |
|---|---|---|
| March/April | Nitrogen | Dried blood 90 (3) or Ammonium sulphate 75 (2½) |
| | Phosphorus | Bone meal 75 (2½) or Superphosphate 45 (1½ |
| | Potassium | Potassium sulphate 75 (2½) or Muriate of potash 45 (1½) |
| | Compost or manure | 2–4 kg per sq metre (4–8lb/sq yd) |
| July *(after* flowering)[**] | Nitrogen | Ammonium sulphate 60 (2) |

[*] Quantities expressed in grams per square metre (oz/sq yd in brackets).
[**] Only necessary in case of weak growth.

## Vine spacing

With the exception of very vigorous varieties such as Baco and Brant, which need about three metres (10ft) between them, all varieties mentioned in this book should be spaced at approximately 1.2m (4ft) intervals. If two or more rows are planted alongside each other, the rows should not be closer than 1.2m, and commercial vineyards usually have their rows separated by 1.5–1.8m (5–6ft) to allow the passage of machinery. Rows planted too closely make working between them difficult and risk encouraging mildews through lack of ventilation.

Theoretically the rows should run north and south so that both sides of the trellis receive an equal amount of sunshine, but in my experience this is quite unimportant.

# ☙ 5 Planting, training and pruning

As far as growth is concerned vines may be conveniently divided into two groups, one having 'normal vigour' and the other 'high vigour'. All the varieties mentioned in this book with the exception of Baco, Brant and Strawberry Grape, are of normal vigour. Training for each type is a little different and so they will be dealt with separately here. The following applies to the normal vigour vine and differences in the treatment of the others will be covered later. For the sake of simplicity, description is restricted to the Guyot system.

## First year

### *Late March or early April*

Planting is normally carried out in the spring although it can be done at any time during the dormant period from the end of November to late April. Some nurseries supply excellent potted or containerised vines, but steer clear of those which have obviously outlived their sell-by date. The soil should be prepared by fertilising and digging over well, before the vines arrive. When the plants do arrive they need not be planted immediately if there is no time, but they should in any case be unpacked and have their roots lightly heeled in under moist, but not sodden, soil. They may be left like this for a few days without coming to any harm from frost or drying out. There is generally no advantage in planting a

16. *Young plants from the nursery – before and after pruning for planting.*

vine of two or three years of age. A one year-old vine will fruit just as quickly because an older vine still has to establish a new root system. Furthermore, a one year-old vine may be trained exactly as you wish from the beginning.

As can be seen from the photograph the plant is very simple at this stage having roots at one end and a small shoot at the other. If you receive a plant with more than one shoot, remove all but the strongest with a sharp pair of secateurs. If the roots are longer than 10cm (4in.), cut them back to this length, and similarly cut the one shoot back to two or three buds. Dig a hole about 30cm (12in.) deep and 30cm in diameter. In the middle of this hole push in a good 1.5–1.8m (5–6ft) bamboo

*17. Young vine after planting.*

and plant the vine against it. Mix a little *well rotted* compost with the top soil portion and ensure that it goes back around the roots, which should be spread out well. The depth at which the roots should be depends on the soil. If it is very heavy the roots should be about 10cm (4in.) deep, but if it is light they should be a little deeper. Do not have them so deep that the shoot is closer than 5cm (2in.) to the soil surface.

The plant should be firmly heeled in as this helps the root development. Unless the soil is very wet, the vine should be watered in.

## May

In this month the buds will swell and burst unless the plant is particularly slow in getting away. When the first of the tiny new shoots is about 2cm (¾in.) long, select the most robust and rub out all others. During this first year you must allow *only one* shoot to grow, the idea being to concentrate the strength of the plant into this new stem. As this new green shoot is so close to the ground in the first year it runs the risk of damage by a late spring frost if there is one. Therefore it is a good idea during this month to keep an eye on the weather forecast, and should there be a frost warning you can cover your young vines with weighted newspapers. This will effectively protect the plants from being nipped and set back a while. The shoot should be loosely but firmly tied to the bamboo every 15cm (6in.) or so to prevent it being damaged by the wind. Twist wired-paper ties are the best kind, but always leave plenty of room for stem expansion. As the leaves grow it will be noticed that a little bud will appear in the axil of each leaf (see photograph).

These buds will break into small lateral shoots and these should be rubbed out at an early stage to prevent them sapping strength from the

*18. Growing shoot showing leaf axils with lateral shoots and dormant bud.*

main stem. A second bud will appear later next to the first. but these should be left untouched as they will develop into the following year's shoots and they will remain dormant this year.

## June to August

The single stem continues to grow and laterals are constantly removed as they appear. This removal of laterals is only done in the first and second year of the life of the vine.

## September

From this month onwards laterals should be allowed to grow on. Towards the end of this month the growing top few inches of the main stem are pinched out to assist the stem to ripen. The length of the stem will depend on the variety, the soil fertility and the type of weather that has been experienced during the summer. It may be as little as six inches or it may be more than sixteen feet. Normally you may expect

*19. Young vines in July of their first year.*

three or four feet of growth. If it is less do not worry because some vines take a little time to find their feet, but at the same time check that you fed the vine with fertilizer, especially if you have a light soil. Of course if growth has been more than 2m (6ft) you cannot continue to grow it upward for ever, so bend it along a horizontal wire at a convenient height and keep tying it down.

## October to December

The vine may now be left alone. The leaves will fall in October and November and by the end of the year you will have nothing but a bare cane.

## Second year

### January and February

The course of action you take now depends on how much wood your vines produced in their first summer. If the cane grew vigorously and you have more than three or four feet of ripe healthy wood as thick as a pencil, then you should proceed as for third year treatment, and you may have a small crop of grapes in the coming summer only eighteen months after you planted the vine. However, it is more normal to find that the first year cane is either rather short or spindly. First of all you must find out how much of the cane is ripe wood because the top will usually have died back a little. Taking a pair of sharp secateurs and working from the top, cut back bud by bud until you reach living dormant wood. This is easily recognised by its pale green inside and brown outside. The outer colour will vary from straw to deep red-brown depending on the variety. When you have reached this point you know that what you have left is healthy wood and it is at this stage that you should decide whether to proceed as for third year treatment or not. It has just been said that the remaining cane is often rather short or spindly, and if this is the case you take your courage in one hand and your secateurs in the other and cut the cane back to only two or three buds. You may wonder what you have achieved in a season. The answer is not only 10cm (4in.) of new cane, it is that the vine has now established

20. Cutting a young vine cane back to establish the extent of healthy, dormant wood.

its roots and in the coming summer it will produce a shoot of much greater vigour which will bear the first crop in the following year.

## April

The buds on the pruned back cane swell.

## May to September

The buds burst in May and you should carry out exactly the same procedure as you did in the first year. One shoot only is allowed to grow

41 ∞

and all laterals are removed until September. At the end of September the growing tip is pinched out as before.

## October to December

The leaves will fall, leaving a bare cane which will, as mentioned before, be much stronger and longer than it was in the first year. The dormant buds along its length will produce the fruiting shoots in the coming year.

## Third year

The principles of pruning are very simple, the two most important facts being firstly that the fruiting shoots always grow from canes grown in the previous year, and secondly it follows that by governing the amount of last year's cane you leave on the vine, you also govern the size of the potential crop. Never be tempted to over-crop your vines; after all, it is no use producing an enormous crop if it doesn't ripen, for loading unripe grape juice with sugar will still make bad wine. The size of the crop you get will depend on several factors such as the year's weather, the vine variety, the vine age and the soil fertility. The first crop your vines bear will be only about half the weight they will bear two years later. Vines taking up only four feet of wire may give as little as two or as much as fifteen pounds of grapes, whereas vigorous vines such as Baco or Brant may give as much as fifty pounds of fruit, although of course a much larger space is needed to bear it. The highest quality wine is produced from normal-vigour vines.

## January and February

You should now inspect your vines and prune each back bud by bud as before, then any cane which is left longer than 1.5m (5ft) should be cut back to that length. If you have a little less than 1.5m (5ft) do not worry.

At this time you should set up your wire trellis. If your vines are planted by a wall or fence make sure that the wires are at least 10cm (4in.) from the wall or fence otherwise the fruit will be liable to damage by wind later. If the vines are planted in the open, the wires should be

*21. Tying down a cane for
the first time.*

stretched between posts set firmly in the ground and stiffened with stays or ground anchors if the rows are to be very long.

A cane-supporting wire (2.5mm) is stretched at a height of 60cm (24in.) above the ground. Over this cane wire are stretched pairs of wires (2mm), each pair having 5–8cm (2–3in), or the thickness of the supporting posts, between them. The first pair is stretched about 24cm (9in.) above the cane wire and further pairs are stretched at 30cm (12in.) intervals up to 1. 5 or 1. 8m (5 or 6ft) above the ground.

Now taking each vine in turn, count ten buds from the point where the cane grows up past the cane wire and cut off the remainder. What is left is bent onto the cane wire, twisted a few times around it and secured at the tip just inside the last bud with a tight tie. If the wire is well tensioned this method makes for a very rigid system which will not move and chafe in the wind. Some care is needed when making the bend which should be fairly tight so that the cane is held firmly in position. A tight bend will also restrict sap flow enough to encourage strong shoots at the top of the vertical part of the cane (the stock), which can be used as replacement canes described below.

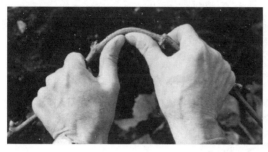

*22. Bending a cane at an internode.*

Bends should be made in the middle of an internode, that is the section of cane between two buds. Bends attempted at nodes will almost certainly result in breakages. The photo above illustrates cane bending which must be done gently but firmly. Grip the cane tightly with both hands almost touching, easing with the thumbs. The cane will frequently creak, but this does no harm. Success comes with practice and it would be a good plan to get this by bending any surplus wood already cut from the vine to get the feel of it. Occasionally a cane will snap no matter how careful you are, but if it only splits halfway through it is still usable and should bear as well as one that is undamaged. If the cane is very thick, or the internodes are very short, it is a good idea to make the total bend over the distance of two internodes, being careful not to put pressure on the node in the middle.

Never be tempted to bend down too much too soon as this will result in weak growth which provides nothing in the way of replacement canes which will be required next year. If in doubt as to the cane's suitability for bending down it is much wiser to cut it off level with the bottom wire and let just the topmost three or four buds break.

## April

The buds along the cane swell.

## May

The buds burst and the fruiting shoots commence growth. Any shoots which appear from the vine within 40cm (15in.) of the ground should be rubbed out. The bottom 40cm or so of the vine will become the permanent stock or trunk of the plant. No further disbudding should be done as you have already fixed the number of fruiting shoots by your pruning. The buds which burst along and just below the cane-wires should be allowed to grow unchecked as fruiting shoots. Removal of shoot laterals is now neither necessary nor advisable.

## June

As the fruiting shoots grow they should be tucked in between the pairs of wires. This keeps the growth neat and allows the maximum penetration of light to the leaves. The pairs of wires may be loosely clipped together if necessary now and then.

Often it is necessary to tie in growth, particularly when the trellis has only single wires. The best and cheapest material to use for this is wire-

*23. Vine flower in bud.*

reinforced paper strip. This is obtainable precut into lengths, 12cm (5in.) being the most suitable. At present these are marketed as *Twist-Ems* or *Fasties* and are stocked by most garden shops. Pass the tie around the shoot and wire, allowing *plenty* of space for growing expansion. Cross the ends of the tie at right angles and twist together three or four times. This instruction might seem a little basic, but I have so often seen shoots cut by too tight a tie, and others break free because the twisting has not been thorough. Do not use the flat plastic-covered wire ties as these have quite sharp edges and can damage green shoots.

During the month, or even during the previous month, the flower buds will appear and gradually become more prominent. The time blossoming actually begins will depend on the variety and the weather, but it is usually in late June or early July. *Under no circumstances* should outdoor vines have their fruiting shoots pinched out a few leaves above the flower as is often suggested in old books. Far from helping the flower to set its fruit this is more likely to throw the flower and give a poor set. The fruiting shoots should be allowed to grow on until they pass the top pair of wires which will not normally be until late July or August. The leaves are the factories of the vine and the farther north the grower is, the more leaves will be needed on the vines to produce the sugar for the fruit. As the flower appears early in summer the crop will always be borne low on the vine.

## July

If flowering did not take place in June it will do so in this month. All the varieties mentioned in this book are self-pollinating, but dry weather is hoped for during the flowering period to assist pollination although a little rain does very little harm. The fruit sets quickly and the tiny young grapes appear and slowly swell.

We sometimes tend to forget that fruit is not produced for our benefit, but for that of the species. Whether we think of apples, acorns or grapes, they are produced only for propagation. It is pure chance that some fruits are palatable purely as an aid to seed dispersal, although we have been able to improve their palatability and fruitfulness by means of breeding and selection over the centuries. But how do fruits arise? Not always as you might think – simply between blossoming and harvest. Most perennials, including vines, take around 15 months to produce a crop.

If we look at our vines in late summer we see only this year's grapes ripening, but next year's have already been initiated and lie hidden as embryo flowers within dormant buds. In the axil of each leaf – that is the angle between the leaf stalk and the stem – there are two buds. One breaks soon after forming, to become a lateral shoot. The other remains dormant until the following season. The word 'dormant' really only describes the outward appearance. Inside, the cells are busy dividing and differentiating into various organs so that the bud soon becomes a highly compressed and packaged shoot complete with leaves and flowers.

Much of this differentiation takes place during the latter half of July and throughout August, in fact the six-week period immediately following the flowering of the current year's blooms. It might justly be said that the vine at this time bears two crops – one as visible grapes, the other invisible as next season's potential crop, which will lie dormant during the coming winter and emerge as next summer's flowers. The number of potential flower clusters within the bud is variable and depends to a great extent on the weather during the differentiation period. If it is warm, many embryo flowers will be formed, but if it is cold, the number will be few. Therefore it will be appreciated that a large crop is not just the result of a good summer in the year it is picked, but also of a good summer the previous year. This was illustrated by the exceptional summers of 1975 and 1976, yielding larger-than-average crops in 1976 and 1977. Fortunately we do not need exceptional summers to give good fruit bud differentiation. The summer of 1979 was by no means special, but the amount of flower borne in 1980 was excellent even though its promise was denied because of poor weather during flowering. This indicates the second condition for a good crop. The weather for pollination and fertilisation must be adequate when the vines finally flower. In this country, this is in late June or, more usually, in the first half of July.

## The flowers

Vine flowers are borne in clusters, between one and three generally being borne on each fruiting shoot. The flowers are an insignificant pale green, and before opening the clusters resemble tiny bunches of grapes. The method by which the flowers open is unusual. The petals do not part from the apex like those of a buttercup, but split from the flower

*24. Vine blossom. Left, in flower. Right, just after fertilisation.*

stalk end towards the apex so that the five petals, still joined, are shed as a little cap or calyptra. The stamens bearing the male, pollen-producing anthers then straighten and elongate. They are arranged around the female ovary consisting of two compartments each containing two ovules, which, once fertilized, become the pips or seeds. Surmounting the ovary is a short style terminating in a stigma which exudes a syrup designed to trap pollen grains and encourage them to 'germinate'. At the base of the ovary, alternating with the stamens, are nectaries but in spite of these, and a light but attractive flower scent, pollination is hardly ever aided by insects.

## Pollination

The optimum requirement for pollination is a warm, dry spell. At such times the anther pollen sacks are more readily desiccated and ruptured to shed their grains. With the assistance of air currents these grains become trapped in the sticky stigmatic fluid and pollination is complete. Fertilisation has yet to take place. It entails the growth of a pollen tube down through the style to an ovule. At least four pollen grains are required to fertilize the four ovules and achieve total success. The more ovules fertilized, the larger will be the grape, all other things being equal. In fact it is common for hundreds of grains to arrive at each stigma, and all compete in the process. Fertilisation is achieved as soon as the grain nuclei unite with those of the ovules, and fruit-set may be said to have taken place. Sometimes a heavy downpour of rain or an unseasonal cold snap during flowering will upset fruit-set and result in bunches containing infertile berries. These will fail to develop and either fall off or remain tiny and hard.

Nearly all vine varieties have self-fertile flowers and do not need pollinators, but a few, particularly some originating in America, have imperfect flowers. This means that they have inadequately developed male or female reproductive organs. If you have a vine of unknown variety and it consistently fails to set fruit it is possible, though uncommon in Britain, that it is one with imperfect flowers. Careful inspection of the flowers with a magnifying glass might enable you to determine this. Flowers lacking properly formed female organs (staminate) exhibit very small or non-existent ovaries. Those with imperfect male organs (pistillate) have stamens which, instead of standing around the ovary like a crown, are curved downwards away from the pistil. In either case self-fertilisation will be poor or impossible.

From all this we can see that a grape crop has two important hurdles to overcome and the critical time is from late June to the end of August. During this period this year's fruit is fertilized and next year's fruit is formed in embryo. If conditions are right for these processes, varieties suitable for our climate will ripen their fruit regardless of the weather during the remainder of the season.

## *August*

Those fruiting shoots that have grown through the top pair of wires should be trimmed off a few inches above the top wire. Ordinary hedge shears will do the job perfectly well. Lateral shoots that stick out untidily may also be trimmed back and mature vines at this time of the year take on the appearance of neat hedges. The fruit will continue to swell and start to ripen towards the end of the month. Ripening begins when white grapes take on a translucency and black grapes begin to colour.

## September

Ripening becomes more marked and early varieties such as Madeleine Angevine and Siegerrebe may become fully ripe in some areas before the end of the month. Bird nets should be put up at the beginning of the month.

## October

Ripening continues to completion and the harvest takes place as soon as the crop is ready. The date you decide upon for your vintage will depend on the variety and the weather. A few extra warm sunny days in the autumn will quickly add a little more sugar to the juice in your grapes, so if the summer has been poorer than average and the autumn is fine, take advantage of it. Only experience can really teach you when you should harvest, and short of pressing a few bunches and using a hydrometer, which is wasteful, or using a refractometer, which is expensive, you will have to rely on your judgement. In southern England or Wales all those varieties mentioned in this book should be ripe by the end of October at the latest unless you happen to live in a particularly cool spot.

As far as tasting for ripeness is concerned *beware!* Different varieties have different levels of juice acidity at the same sugar content. For example Mueller-Thurgau juice is low in acidity compared with Seyval Blanc and if you taste a Mueller-Thurgau grape of say 18% sugar and then a Seyval Blanc grape of 18%, the latter will not taste as sweet even though the sugar content is the same. Experience alone with the varieties you grow will enable you to estimate the approximate degree of ripeness by tasting.

Always try to harvest your grapes in dry weather. Not only is it much more comfortable but rain will reduce the gravity of the juice and dilute the flavour. Grape bunches can carry a lot of water between the berries and obviously this is undesirable in the must. If you use secateurs for the harvest *take care!* It is so easy after picking for a while, to become careless and take a finger tip off. If you can obtain them, get hold of a pair of grape-cutting shears. These can still give you a nip but they will do no serious damage. On no account pick grapes that you cannot process the same day. Once grapes have been taken from the vine they will begin to deteriorate due to wild yeast ferments and juice oxidation.

## November and December

Leaf fall takes place and the vine is left to ripen its wood.

## Fourth year

### January and February

You have now reached the stage when you will carry out winter pruning as it should be carried out year after year. If pruning were not carried out the vine would grow larger every year but it would bear a crop that would never ripen. Winter pruning is designed to keep the vine both in shape and from growing larger and larger. The vine will now appear rather like that shown in the photo.

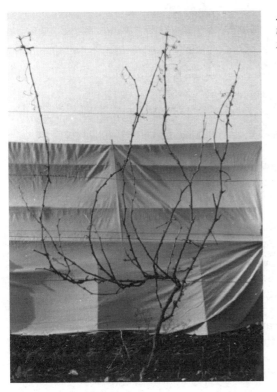

*25. Vine at the end of its third year – before pruning.*

*26. Vine at the end of its third year – after pruning before bending down.*

What you must do now is to replace the old cane you bent onto the cane-bearing wires last year with new cane. Ideally, instead of replacing it with one long cane it is better to replace it with two short canes bent down onto the cane-bearing wires in opposite directions. This system of pruning is called 'double guyot'. Replacement canes are chosen for their quality as well as their position. They should be neither too thin nor too thick, the ideal diameter for most varieties being 7–10mm (¼–⅜in.). If they are very spindly they will probably have poor fruit potential, and if too heavy will bend badly. The optimum internode length is about 10cm (4in.), but this is not so important. Having selected your two replacement canes for bending down onto the bearer wire, remove the old arms on this wire and all other canes, except maybe for the short spur near the stock. This should result in the vine looking like that shown in the photograph.

*27. Vine at the end of its third year – after pruning and bending down.*

The two canes are each cut back to10 buds and they are bent down onto, and are twisted around, the cane-bearing wires as shown in the photo, their ends being firmly tied. Do not worry if they overlap the neighbouring vines. Experience over the years will tell you the optimum number of buds to tie down in order to balance the growth potential of the vine. Too few buds will result in excess vigour and unruly growth; too many buds will result in weak shoots and possibly too great a crop to ripen properly. Each bud is, after all, going to produce a fruit-bearing shoot. If your vines are reasonably robust try tying down a total of 20 buds and adjust in future if required.

The short spur is left mainly to increase the chances of good replacement canes growing near the stock, although the shoots it produces will usually carry fruit too. Spurs are selected if possible from canes which spring from the old wood of the stock and their main object is to keep

*28. Vine at the end of its fourth year – before pruning.*

*29. Vine at the end of its fourth year – after pruning ready for bending down.*

*30. Young vines of fruiting age in June.*

*31. Mature vines being tied in and summer pruned in August.*

the vine in shape, for it will be readily understood that if you constantly take replacement canes from the previous year's *main* canes these replacements will spring farther and farther from the stock each year. Therefore we utilise the periodical appearance of 'watersprouts' or shoots from the old stock, to reshape the vine as required. After a few years, the top of the vine stock will tend to become enlarged and be a plentiful source of replacement canes.

Every year from now on you should carry out double guyot pruning as described above. The best time of the year for this operation is in January or February. At this time the vine is properly dormant. If the vine is pruned too late in spring it will 'bleed' sap. This is not really serious although it used to be thought so, nevertheless it is best avoided if possible. Also canes which are not bent down onto the cane-wires before bud burst will throw most of their growth at the cane extremities.

## Training high-vigour vines

Vigorous varieties such as Baco and Brant need much more room than others. As a result it is convenient to train them and prune them differently, the main difference being that instead of having a small permanent stock they have a large permanent framework on which there are several spurs.

During the first two years of the life of these vines, training is little different from the procedure described for normal-vigour vines. If a sturdy cane is grown in the first year it is cut back only to the height at which you wish the fruit to be carried. If you are growing these vines on a house, this height will be determined by such features as windows and doors. If growth is weak in the first year cut the vine back to a few buds and in the second year allow only one bud to develop so that the desired height will then be achieved as in Fig. 2.

In the following summer the top five or six buds are allowed to grow as fruiting shoots, all other buds lower down being rubbed out as in Fig. 3.

At the end of the year the two sturdiest canes are selected and bent horizontally in opposite directions. You will have to use your judgement as to their length. They should start at around six feet each although in later years they may be extended up to 10 feet.

These arms will form a permanent part of the vine frame but for the

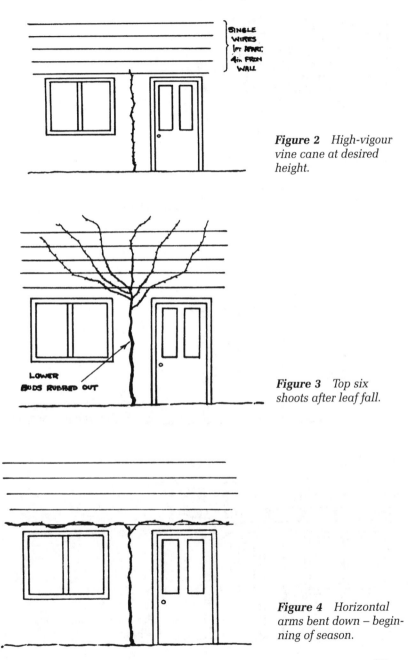

SINGLE
WIRES
1FT APART
4in FROM
WALL

*Figure 2*   *High-vigour vine cane at desired height.*

LOWER
BUDS RUBBED OUT

*Figure 3*   *Top six shoots after leaf fall.*

*Figure 4*   *Horizontal arms bent down – beginning of season.*

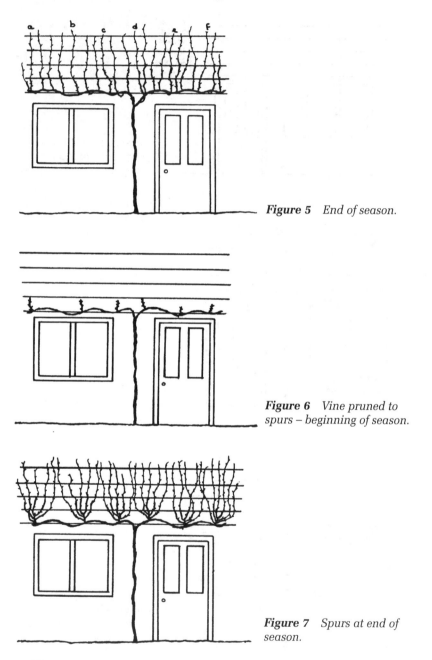

**Figure 5**   *End of season.*

**Figure 6**   *Vine pruned to spurs – beginning of season.*

**Figure 7**   *Spurs at end of season.*

first year of their life every bud along their length will become a fruiting shoot so that by the end of the season the vine will appear something like Fig. 5.

So far training has been only a slight variation of the normal-vigour vine procedure, but from now on instead of replacing each arm of the vine every winter a number of spurs is left along each arm. In Fig. 5 canes a, b, c, d, e and f have been selected to be cut back to four or five buds while the remaining canes are completely removed. The distance between spurs should be about two feet, and after pruning the vine will look like Fig. 6.

In the following spring all the buds on the spurs will develop into fruiting shoots as in Fig. 7 and in the next winter, and every winter after that, the strongest cane from each spur is cut back to four or five buds as a replacement while all the others are removed as in Fig. 8.

From time to time watersprout canes can be used to provide new spurs and keep the vine in shape.

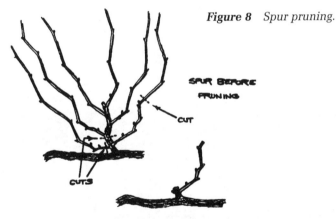

*Figure 8*    *Spur pruning.*

SPUR BEFORE
PRUNING

CUT

CUTS

SPUR AFTER PRUNING

# ‫ℂ 6  Vine pests and maladies

The vine, like all plants, is susceptible to certain ailments and pests although there is no reason why any of them should cause the grower serious concern as long as sensible precautions are taken. All the hazards likely to be met in England are discussed below and the means to combat them is given.


## Mildews

There are several mildews which attack the vine from time to time but fortunately they may be easily and cheaply prevented by a sensible spraying programme. Growers who suffer serious damage to their vines due to bad mildew only have themselves to blame. There are three forms of mildew which are more common than any others and happily the treatment we use to prevent them also effectively prevents the others.

Downy mildew or peronospora *(Plasmopara viticola)* affects both the leaves, which turn brown and die, and the fruit which shrivel and become leathery in appearance. The German name for this disease is *lederbeeren* which means literally 'leather berry', and grapes infected with this fungus will not ripen. The old form of treatment was Bordeaux mixture and it is still used in some parts of Europe, but one of its disadvantages is that every application retards vine growth for up to three days and obviously if several applications are made throughout the season, the vine growth may be retarded for a fortnight. Modern treatments often retard growth less and employ materials such as *Dithane 945*. Downy mildew is not very common in Britain because it is encouraged by warm, wet conditions. Our climate is usually cool and wet or warm and dry.

However it is most unwise to ignore the possibility of an outbreak because so much damage can be done if vines are infected. There is also the likelihood of a similar mildew, rote brenner *(Pseudopeziza tracheiphila)* which favours the cool wet weather we frequently experience in the spring. The most obvious symptoms are brown leaf patches which turn quite red before withering. Fortunately the fungicide already mentioned will deal with both diseases.

A mildew requiring a different fungicide is oidium or powdery mildew *(Uncinula necator)* (see the photograph). This disease affects all

**Figure 9**   *Grapes infected with peronospera.*

*32. Powdery mildew (oidium) on grapes – note the dusty appearance and splitting berries.*

parts of the plant. The first sign on grapes is a white dusty appearance followed by splitting and blackening of the berries. No further ripening will take place. Sulphur effectively prevents oidium, but it is wiser to use a wettable form as opposed to Flowers of Sulphur which if applied too heavily can cause leaf burn. Baco is sulphur-shy and should not be sprayed with sulphur but, in any case, it is resistant to oidium.

A most effective remedy for oidium is *Rubigan*, obtainable from agricultural merchants. This compound not only prevents the disease, but will actually cure it in its earliest stages. *Murphy's Systemic Fungicide* is also quite effective.

This compound will also prevent *botrytis* or grey mould. Most people are familiar with it on such fruit as strawberries. By keeping other mildews in check and also by keeping the vines healthy by feeding them correctly, the risk of *botrytis* infection is much reduced as this fungus cannot penetrate the skin of the grape unless it is first damaged by some other agent. The most common symptoms of *botrytis* are the bunch stems turning brown and drying up, causing premature bunch drop, and the berries turning pinkish grey and growing fuzzy coats of mould. *Botrytis* is undesirable on red grapes at any time as it destroys the red pigment in the skin, but white grapes destined for winemaking do not suffer badly as long as they are infected when they are reasonably ripe. As already mentioned, certain wines such as the French Sauternes and the German Auslesen actually depend on this fungus infecting their

**Figure 10**   *Grapes infected with botrytis.*

grapes to produce their beautiful flavour. Provided your grapes are moist inside when you pick them do not discard them, however revoltingly rotten they may look! If, on the other hand, part of the bunch is quite dry it should be cut out or it will impart a musty taste to the wine.

Although infected berries may be used, the juice yield will be diminished and for this reason, if for no other, it is sensible to take every precaution to prevent infection. The disease can spread very rapidly and lead to complete crop spoilage. Dessert grapes will, of course, be ruined by attack at any stage. *Botrytis* spores are ever-present in the air and they can attack any damaged vine tissue under almost any conditions, though moist weather, particularly if accompanied by wide differences between day and night temperatures, is the most dangerous.

Dead-arm (*Phomopsis viticola*) used to be considered of minor importance, but it now appears to be more of a menace than was once supposed. Vines in a weakened state due to a waterlogged soil or nutrient deficiency, are most vulnerable, but when climatic conditions suit the disease it can appear anywhere. Ripened canes in the winter show a silvering of the bark and are peppered with tiny black specks (not to be confused with the larger lumpy black spots of *Botrytis sclerotes* overwintering bodies). If the infection is light no other symptoms may appear, but often buds fail to break in the spring and whole canes may die back. Liquid copper used during the summer will help harden the plant tissue and prevent attack. Winter wash with a product such as *Ovamort* or *Mortegg* will also help, but I must confess to being in two minds about winter washes. They undoubtedly clean the dormant wood of pests and diseases, but they also kill hibernating predators such as ladybirds which often infest the vine bark. In our vineyard we decided against winter wash, but I do not think one can be pedantic about it.

A very unpleasant, but fortunately uncommon, mildew is *Penicillium*. I have only seen it twice in eighteen years, and then only locally, but grapes showing signs of it must be discarded. If used for winemaking very strong off-flavours can appear. The mould usually appears associated with *botrytis*, but unlike the grey fuzz of *botrytis*, *penicillium* is sky-blue.

## Mildew prevention by spraying

Mildew must be prevented rather than cured, for once it has got a hold it is usually impossible to do more than control further spread of the disease. Failure to carry out a sensible spraying programme is very likely to lose you your crop, and vines which are infected badly year after year may soon be destroyed.

In 1971 many growers in Spain must have bitterly regretted not having sprayed, because that summer mildew reduced the Spanish wine output to a trickle. Normally being very dry there they do not expect mildew trouble and do not spray very often, but in that year they paid the price. In our far more humid conditions it is simply asking for trouble not to spray preventatively. Peronospera and *botrytis* must be guarded against all season, and although oidium is only supposed to be dangerous in hot weather, with our variable climate it is sensible to spray for this disease just as often.

Vines are open to attack from the moment of budburst until the end of the season, and it is wise to be prepared for the worst and assume that all the mildews are just waiting for a chance to take advantage of the lazy grower. If you do get mildew in your vines it is nearly always due to laziness because the simplified spray programme given in the table below is really very little trouble. *All* parts should be sprayed.

Apply at the rate recommended by the manufacturer at 10 to 20 day intervals from late April (budburst) to early October (cease at least two weeks before harvest). Unless specifically advised, most fungicides may be mixed and applied together. For obvious reasons the wetter the weather the more frequent the spraying should be. Ideally this should be carried out on a dry day with dry weather forecast, but do not keep

**Fungicidal spray programme for the prevention of mildew**

| Malady | Conditions most favouring development | Fungicide |
|---|---|---|
| Downy mildew | Warm and wet | Murphy's Liquid Copper or Cuprokylt or Dithane 945 |
| Rote brenner | Cool and wet | As for downy mildew |
| Botrytis | Any damp weather | Murphy's Systemic, Elvaron |
| Dead-arm | Cool and wet | Murphy's Systemic, Cuprokylt |
| Powdery mildew | Hot and dry but humid | Sulphur, Rubigan, Top-Cop |

Cuprokylt, Dithane 945m Elvaron, Rubigan and Top-Cop are obtainable from agricultural merchants putting off spraying in a prolonged damp spell. If the fungicides are on the vines for no more than twelve hours before being washed off by more rain they will at least take care of spores then emerging, and some spray will stick on under the leaves for a longer period.

In the past it was unwise to spray during flowering because the earlier chemicals used could upset the blossom. *It is still unwise to apply copper during flowering,* but most modern compounds are safe if applied at the proper rate with a fine mist nozzle.

## Insects and related pests

### Phylloxera

In England we have a tremendous advantage over the continental grower in that one of the worst pests of all is not endemic here. This pest is *Phylloxera vestatrix,* a little aphid with a very complicated life cycle and a disastrous effect on the European vine on the continent. The only effective method of fighting this pest is to plant only grafted vines which have resistant rootstocks, as the most dangerous attack is to the roots. The extra cost of grafted vines is rather a waste of money as far as the English amateur is concerned as the chances of *phylloxera* ever establishing itself here are remote. The climate is generally unsuitable and the vineyards too widely spaced to encourage spread.

More importantly, it is the policy of our Ministry of Agriculture, Fisheries and Food to keep our shores free of this pest by means of the compulsory destruction of any infected plants.

In the dozen appearances that have occurred in England in the past one hundred years all have been stamped out at source. Destruction would also apply to grafted vines because although they can tolerate the pest, they can still harbour it. I am in total agreement with this policy on the grounds that it is sheer stupidity to admit any pest into Britain if we can avoid it. Apart from the dangers of the insect itself, it almost certainly acts as a vector for virus diseases. Government policy renders the use of grafted vines in this country an irrelevance, except as an insurance policy for commercial growers in the event of a change in that policy – indeed grafted vines suffer several disadvantages.

Ungrafted plants are highly adaptable regarding soil types and will live and bear well for centuries, whereas grafted vines need carefully selected rootstocks to suit different soils, and they may need to be uprooted and replaced after about twenty years due to graft failure. They also suffer more under conditions of stress and are more expensive. Our vineyard was about half grafted and half ungrafted, the latter consistently performing better.

Although you are most unlikely to ever see *phylloxera*, you should be aware of the symptoms. As already said, the aphid spends most of its life, and does all its serious damage, under soil, where roots may exhibit nodules due to injury. However, under suitable conditions the pest goes through a wandering aerial stage when it climbs up into the foliage and causes blister-like galls on the leaves particularly those of hybrid varieties. These blisters appear on the underside of the leaf, and should not be confused with the gall of the erineum mite (see below) which occurs on the upperside.

## *Red spider*

Occasional and isolated attacks by this mite may be experienced but they are easily treated by spraying with any suitable insecticide obtainable from your garden shop. It is wise to spray insecticides only when and where you have to, because of course both harmful and beneficial insects are destroyed. The usual symptoms of red spider attack are malformed growing shoots and lace-like brown-edged holes in the leaves. Mild attack is unimportant and may be ignored.

## *Wasps*

In the average year wasps are of little concern as the grapes ripen after the wasps have started to decline in numbers. However, if you have an early variety or the summer and autumn has been particularly favourable for wasps, these insects can be very troublesome. The only really effective treatment is to find the offending nests and destroy them but this is seldom possible. The old-fashioned trick of putting down jars of water and jam or beer and vinegar can be most effective, but it will not stop attack of the grapes completely. Do not be tempted to put polythene bags over the grapes for although you may keep the wasps off you will almost certainly get bad mildew instead!

## Erineum mite

As already mentioned, this mite gives rise to blisters on the upperside of leaves. Under the leaf each blister exhibits a minor cavity, often covered with a grey-white felt-like mat. Generally damage is insignificant, but if you are worried a light dusting with sulphur powder soon puts an end to the problem.

## Rabbits

If you live in the country where rabbits abound you will doubtless be fully aware of the damage they can do to plants. Mature vines are not quite so likely to be attacked but young vines are very attractive to these animals, and one-inch mesh wire netting should either be put around each vine or around the area.

## Deer

Many parts of the country have a surprisingly high population of wild deer, and where present they create a formidable problem. If deer have access to your land the only answer is a wire net fence eight feet high!

## Birds

In the large open commercial vineyards in England birds can be an enormous problem. In the garden, however, it is a simple matter to net your vine area and be protected completely. As it is not necessary to put up the nets until the beginning of September and they are taken down when you pick around the middle of October, the nets will last for years if handled carefully. If you decide on a particularly large planting, or if netting is for some reason impracticable, you will have to resort to a number of deterrents. Most deterrents are effective for a while but birds will get used to anything, so scaring devices such as bangers, coloured balloons and tinsel must be changed every other day. The most troublesome birds are blackbirds, songthrushes and mistlethrushes, and the most vulnerable grapes are the black varieties.

## Failure to produce flower

Vines grown from pips are hardly ever worth the effort, one of their faults sometimes being that they are sterile (and in any case never come true to variety), but known varieties also on occasions produce no flowers. This can be a temporary fault due to unusually bad weather during the flower bud differentiation period of the previous summer. Excessive foliar vigour due to soil over-rich in nitrogen may also discourage flower production. This effect can be aggravated by a deficiency of potash or phosphorus.

## Failure to set fruit

Plants sometimes bear abundant flowers which then fail to set. This may be due to withering of the blossom by *botrytis* or cold, wet weather causing 'coulure'. In this case the pollen is either washed from the flower by heavy rain or the temperature is too low to allow the pollen nuclei to migrate to the ovules. Lastly the vine may be one with imperfect flowers, which are either incapable of being fertilized or require a pollinator variety nearby.

## Weed control

Any plants growing among vines offer competition for the available nutrients, water, light and air. A little light weed cover is of no significance except that it prevents the soil warming up and so has an effect on the air temperature, but some weeds propagate rapidly and others become very large quite quickly, and it is wise to prevent any growth at all if possible. If you have time you can weed and hoe by hand, but many of us have a hundred-and-one other things to do without spending hours weeding. Fortunately there are now several excellent herbicides which if used sensibly keep your vines free of weeds safely.

Before mentioning the right herbicides to use I should point out those which should be avoided at all times. Obviously you should never use compounds such as sodium chlorate because this will permeate through the soil and kill everything whose roots it contacts. The so-called hormone-type weedkillers such as 2,4,D or worse 2,4-5,T should never be used anywhere near vines which are susceptible to fumes. These might be given off for several days from a treated area many yards away. Fumes from a neighbour's lawn which has been treated with a selective herbicide cause symptoms which are usually more horrific in appearance than dangerous, but the problem should be avoided if possible. Leaves exhibiting shrivelled, fan-like distortions with multi-toothed margins are typical signs of damage from one of this family of weedkillers. The effects are usually not permanent, fresh leaves appearing after the fumes have dispersed, reverting to their normal shape, but damage at critical times of the year could prove serious in upsetting the vine's flowering.

This leaves us with three herbicide types which used in combination should answer all our problems. Paraquat/diquat herbicides such as gramaxone, available to the gardener as *Weedol* will affect any green plant growth it touches, but will not be harmful if it touches bark. It acts in the presence of light, working fastest on sunny days. It is not residual

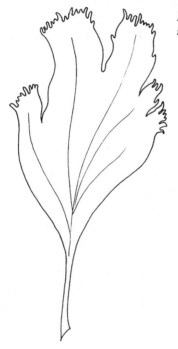

**Figure 11**  *Leaf showing symptoms of selective weedkiller damage.*

and is quickly broken down by soil organisms, but is highly toxic if taken into the mouth. It kills annuals, but only burns off the tops of perennials which regrow later. Persistent use of this compound alone would eventually encourage perennials by means of eliminating annual competition. Perennials can be eliminated by using glyphosate herbicide, available as *Tumbleweed* or *Roundup*. This is expensive but very effective if applied to weeds with a good leaf area in active growth. Like paraquat it is not residual, but unlike paraquat it is non-toxic to humans and animals.

There are several pre-emergence herbicides which, when applied to the soil surface, prevent weed seeds germinating. While extremely useful in some circumstances, I am opposed to the use of any residual herbicide if possible. Such herbicides should never be used in light soils because instead of being bound near the surface, they can be leached downwards to affect deeper roots, including those of the vine. Even in heavy soils persistent use should be avoided.

Never use mist sprayers for herbicide application. Use either a fine rose or dribble-bar on a watering can or a *Polijet* low pressure fan nozzle on a knapsack sprayer. If paraquat is applied in early spring, the perennials will have made enough regrowth for the effective application of glyphosphate in May or June. Once rid of weeds it is a simple matter to prevent their re-establishment by spot treatment of the appropriate herbicide as required. It is a classical case of the 'stitch in time'. The more weeds become established the harder they are to clear. Remember the old saying 'one year's seeds, seven years weeds'.

# ଓ 7 Propagation

The only way to propagate a vine variety is by some form of form of cutting. Seeds never come true and seedlings, as explained before, almost always produce poorer vines than their parents. There are all sorts of weird and wonderful methods of propagation recommended but only one is worth spending any time on, and that is the 'long cutting' method. Two requirements are necessary: first, light soil and secondly, good cutting material. Do not be tempted to propagate from wood of some unknown variety just because it has been given to you. There is a great likelihood of it being some utterly unsuitable variety.

Cuttings should be of two or three buds and 20–30cm (9–12in.) in length. The wood must be healthy, ripe and sturdy. Black lumps on the outside of the wood indicate the winter spore clusters of *botrytis* mildew and such wood should be destroyed. The cutting should be trimmed so that the bottom cut is made just below a bud. This trimming to size is best done at winter pruning time in January or February, but they should be stored under moist but light soil until late March to protect them from drying out and the frost. In March they are set the right way up in light soil so that the top bud is about two inches above the surface, and they should be heeled in firmly. The cuttings remain in this position for a growing season. Provided they are of good quality, the soil is light and you avoid mildews and nematodes a good percentage should strike roots and put out shoots. They may be lifted either in November or early next spring and planted in their final position. It must be remembered, of course, that whereas a rooted vine will bear fruit only two and a half years after planting, starting from a cutting will take a year longer.

Grafting is really beyond all but the most dedicated amateurs as it requires great skill and special equipment such as heated propagating boxes. For reasons already mentioned, grafting offers no advantages to the amateur in Britain.

# ⊗ 8  Vines in pots or tubs

Those of us fortunate enough to have gardens tend to forget that many either have no garden at all, or possibly only one the size of a pocket handkerchief. Others have the space but only in the shape of a slab of concrete. The colossal sales of growbags in recent years has emphasised this point, and has enabled us to turn barren corners into verdant mini-jungles. I would not recommend any perennial be grown in a growbag, but patios and courtyards are brightened up with pots and tubs, and these can be used for grapevines.

Naturally you cannot grow a vine to its normal size unless the container is very large, but if the plant is kept to a size proportional to the volume of its holder there is no reason why you should not produce some prime grapes. There is, of course, no upper limit to the size of the container, and I would not like to be specific regarding the lower limit, but for practical purposes it is probably not worthwhile using anything less than a 12-inch pot. Even then you should not expect to get more than a couple of bunches a year. At the other end of the scale a hogs-head barrel cut in half will provide homes for two quite sizeable plants yielding sensible crops.

All containers should be thoroughly cleaned before filling. Drainage holes should be provided if not already present. Tubs should have 2.5cm (1in.) holes bored at intervals of about 20cm (8in.) in the base, and the whole container should then be treated well with a wood pre-servative. Some brands are unsuitable for use in close proximity to plants, but *Cuprinol* supply a suitable grade in their range.

**Figure 12**  *Mature vine in tub.*

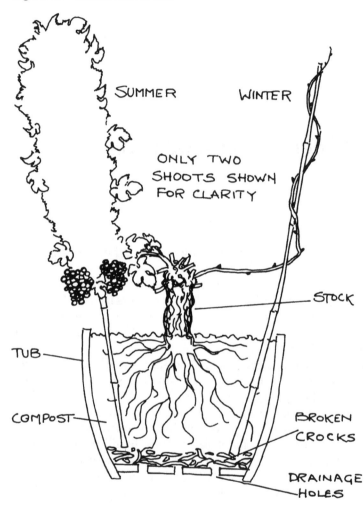

Before filling the container make sure that it is either in its final position or can easily be moved on wheels or castors when full, or you may find yourself with an immovable tub a long way from its proposed site. Place a layer of broken crocks over the drain holes to prevent clogging and then top up with the growing medium. The nature of this material is critical. The vine's health will largely be governed by the amount of water and nutrients present. Both must be available in sufficiency, but not in excess.

This is really the nub of the matter and the smaller the volume of soil, the more difficult it is to maintain the balance of the conditions in it. If too much fertilizer is applied to a garden bed it is usually fairly soon absorbed by the great mass of soil and leached out, but in a confined container it can remain at a toxic level for an extended period and cause serious damage to the occupying plant. Similarly the moisture content is liable to rapid and wide variation unless the compost is of the right consistency. Remember that your vine is going to have to live out its life in the same cramped home and if the soil is sick it cannot escape by reaching out for a healthier foothold. It is worth the trouble of making up a compost that drains freely while retaining a satisfactory water content and nutrient level. A mixture of one part sharp sand, two parts peat and four parts good loam should provide the desired characteristics.

At the outset you may wish to mix in some fertilizer such as *John Innes* base fertilizer at 3 or 4 oz/bushel (100g/30l), but if in doubt cut this rate down and supplement with a fortnightly liquid feed. Liquid feed will become necessary anyway because any added fertilizer will eventually become exhausted. Don't overdo feeding – it is easier to boost a weak vine than save one being poisoned by a toxic nutrient level.

During the first year of the vine's life only one shoot should be grown, all others being pinched out. If this shoot proves to be weak cut it back at the end of the year and repeat the performance in the following season. If, on the other hand, it is strong and the thickness of a pencil at a height of 30cm (12in.) cut it back to that height during the winter. This growth will become the permanent stock. Two shoots may be allowed in the second year and they may fruit though it is more usual to take the first crop in the third summer. In the second winter cut back again leaving as many buds as you think the vine is capable of bearing shoots in the following season. (Fruiting shoots always spring from the past summer's growth.)

Each subsequent winter, carry out the same treatment leaving more or less buds according to the vigour of the vine. A vine in a 12-inch pot should be allowed to produce only one or two fruiting shoots each year, but a plant in a large tub may bear as many as a dozen shoots or more. Only experience with your particular container, vine variety and compost will tell you just how large your vine may be allowed to develop. To start with err on the mean side – allow fewer shoots rather than more.

After all, it is better to have four plump, ripe bunches, than a dozen undersized clusters of sour green 'peas'. Sometimes it may be helpful to pinch out some flowers if the blooms are very numerous in order to ensure a high leaf-area to fruit-weight ratio.

Training is largely a matter of choice. Some sort of support for the growing shoots must be provided, but the form of support can be arranged to suit the surroundings. A plant in a 12-inch pot will probably be happy with a single five-foot cane up which to train the two shoots each summer, while a vine in a tub will require several canes arranged around the circumference of the tub in goblet form. Alternatively, the vine may first be trained in standard form with a very high stock of over 90cm (3ft) instead of the normal 30cm. The shoots springing from the head of the stock can then be allowed to hang freely unless in a windy position. Whatever training method is used the growing shoots should be stopped at about 120cm (4ft). If the shoots do not make four feet it is probably a sign that you have tried to grow too many, but if four feet is easily achieved and vigorous regrowth follows stopping, you should allow more shoots in the following season.

Apart from the attractiveness of vines grown in this way some excellent, if limited, quantities of fruit may be cropped, but never forget that the performance of any plant in a container will depend on the attention you pay to its condition.

# cs 9  Vines under glass or plastic

Vines have been grown under glass for dessert use in this country for centuries, and you will find listed here varieties recommended for this purpose, but there is nothing to prevent those in colder regions from growing wine under cover. Polythene tunnels have been used to great effect in the production of wine where outdoor culture is not possible. Training and pruning for wine under polythene need be no different from that already described, but the size and shape of some coldhouses do not lend themselves to the Guyot system and this chapter covers more conventional training methods.

The object of a greenhouse or conservatory is to provide an artificially warm climate so that plants otherwise unsuited to cope with our latitudes can be made to thrive and bear crops. In practice this widens considerably the number of grapevines we can grow, and pushes farther north the limits of vine culture. Indeed, a greenhouse situated in the most northerly extremes of Britain will ripen many varieties without the need to resort to artificial heat. The factor that decides whether a variety is for outdoor or glasshouse culture is the local climate. There is no point whatsoever in growing a vine under glass if it will produce good fruit outside – it is merely a waste of house space. On the other hand, it is pointless trying to crop a vine outdoors if it is only suited to house culture in your area – it will grow perfectly happily, but it will not ripen its grapes. Mueller-Thurgau will ripen very well every season outdoors in southern counties, will benefit from a wall north of the Wash and will often need the protection of glass north of Yorkshire.

From this, it will be seen that one cannot be specific when classifying grapes according to their form of culture. Of course there are many vines which will only do well under glass even in the south, though they may be perfectly happy in the open in Spain or Italy. Some varieties are so demanding as to require a little supplied heat, particularly early in the season, but the cost of heating is now so exorbitant as to make the culture of such exotics an expensive luxury. This is especially true when there are so many vines which will give excellent results in an unheated house, so I shall confine myself to these here.

One normally associates the glasshouse with dessert grapes, but there is no reason why those living in the colder parts of the country should not grow grapes for wine inside and a list of predominantly wine-producing varieties was given in Chapter 3.

It is true that the very best quality dessert fruit require glass in our climate, though not for climatic reasons alone. The appearance of first-class dessert fruit is important and a greenhouse eliminates any chance of imperfections due to weather damage.

The following is far from comprehensive but gives a range of varieties suitable for the greenhouse.

## Greenhouse varieties – white

### Golden Chasselas

A very popular, fine flavoured grape with golden, translucent berries. One of the earliest, ripening outdoors in warm summers in good sites.

### Mireille

Early, muscat flavoured, large berries.

### Buckland Sweetwater

Early, prolific, well flavoured variety with heavy bunches of pale amber grapes.

## Foster's Seedling

A free setting, early, very juicy grape of good flavour.

## Lady Hutt

A vigorous mid-season grape. Flavour excellent.

## Mrs Pearson

Similar characteristics to Lady Hutt, but ripening a little later.

## Muscat of Alexandria

Very fine flavour, but requiring hand pollination with varieties such as Black Hamburg or Foster's Seedling. Also only recommended for culture in the south without additional heat.

### Greenhouse varieties – black

## Black Hamburg

The most popular black coldhouse vine in the country with very large black berries. It sets fruit very well and is highly recommended – though *not* for outdoors as is still sometimes advocated. The famous Hampton Court vine is of this variety.

## Muscat Hamburg

A quality muscat grape which ripens a little later than Black Hamburg. It benefits from the presence of another pollinator variety.

*33. Black Hamburg.*

## Mrs Pince

A vigorous, mid-season, fine grape benefiting from hand pollination.

## Muscat Champion

A mid-season, red berried grape which sets quality grapes freely.

## Alicante

A late season vigorous variety requiring hard pruning.

## Types of house

Greenhouses fall into three main categories. The warmest is a south-facing lean-to backing on to a wall. The wall acts as a heat store, trapping

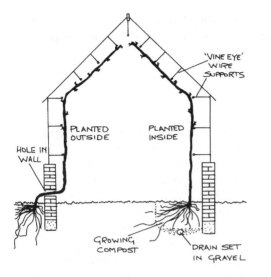

'VINE EYE' WIRE SUPPORTS

PLANTED OUTSIDE

PLANTED INSIDE

HOLE IN WALL

GROWING COMPOST

DRAIN SET IN GRAVEL

**Figure 13** *Greenhouse layout showing vines trained to vertical arms.*

solar energy during the day and releasing it at night. This greatly reduces the temperature variation and makes it possible to grow particularly fussy varieties which need extra warmth. Free-standing, span glasshouses (Fig. 13) are the type most commonly seen. They retain less heat at night, but are perfectly adequate for many varieties. Indeed the even less heat-retentive polythene tunnel will be perfectly suitable for most of the house vines normally found in Britain.

The main restriction on house suitability is that of size. Some grapes are very vigorous, and these should only be grown in the medium to large size garden greenhouse. Others can be reasonably restricted and grown in the smallest houses. Remember that the greenhouse climate encourages more vigorous growth than that normally experienced outside. The size of the vine must be firmly controlled by hard pruning. This need for space is increased by the necessity of having ample room between the supporting wires and the glass or polythene. Foliage in contact with the house can be scorched by the sun or mildewed due to condensation trapped between leaf and glass. With frequent and careful attention the wires can be as close as 30cm (12in.) to the glass, but failure to tie in and pinch out excessive growth constantly will lead to trouble at this spacing, and a gap of 45cm (18in.) is much safer. Methods of fixing the wires will depend on the construction of the house, but only galvanised wire of at least 2.5mm diameter should be used, and it must be firmly secured under reasonable tension. When you set it up try to picture the weight of a mature vine bearing a heavy crop – after all, that is your aim!

## Planting

Vines may be planted either inside or outside the house. Traditionally, the plant is rooted outside and then led through a hole in the footing wall into the house. The object is to leave the floor of the house available for other crops and make the vine find its nutrients and water elsewhere. Alternatively, the vine may be planted in the border of the house itself. Vines rooted outside the house may be planted in the same way as normal outdoor varieties, but rather more preparation must be done to a house border before planting inside. It is not easy maintaining a good soil structure under cover because normal weathering is prevented and moisture must be added by artificial means, often employing hard water from the mains. The growing medium should be such that it retains nutrients and water without becoming waterlogged. This requires either the presence of a naturally free-draining soil underneath or artificial drains.

A good base for the border may be mixed from three parts loam, one part coarse sand and one part peat. Manure may be liberally forked in, but it must be well rotted. Its function is more one of soil conditioner than supplier of nutrients. Too much fertilizer will only encourage sappy growth at the expense of fruit potential. Tales of horses buried under vines are rife but that requirement is quite fallacious! The fertilizer needs of the greenhouse vine are much the same as those described for outdoor plants in Chapter 4, but allowances should be made for the size of the vine and its root spread.

The spacing of vines depends very much on how large you intend each plant to grow. You may have one vine eventually taking up an entire house, or you may decide on the greater interest of several smaller vines of various varieties. Within the limits of the vine's natural vigour, the house microclimate will allow you to prune your plants to the size you require.

## Training

During the first year the plant is treated exactly as if it were an outdoor vine. Only one strong bud is allowed to develop into a shoot and all laterals are pinched out to assist the leader. It is normal practice to train house-vines on the spur pruning principle. The permanent arms carrying the spurs may be horizontal or vertical (Fig. 14). If you intend to train horizontal arms the method is precisely the same as that employed for outdoor high-vigour vines already described. The alternative vertical arm is extended to its full length in the same manner, but is led straight to the peak of the house. Wood selected during winter pruning for arm extension should be at least the thickness of a pencil. Never be tempted to tie in weak canes – in the long run they will only increase the time required to grow the vine to its desired size and shape.

**Figure 14**  *House vines after winter pruning to spurs on permanent arms.*

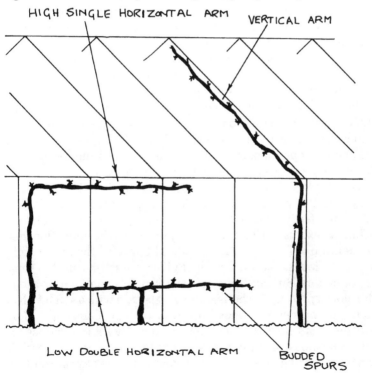

HIGH SINGLE HORIZONTAL ARM    VERTICAL ARM

LOW DOUBLE HORIZONTAL ARM    BUDDED SPURS

The formation period of the vine arm, or arms, will vary depending on the fertility of the soil and the natural vigour of the vine variety. A vine with two short horizontal arms or one vertical arm may be fully shaped in two seasons, or it may take three or even four seasons to reach its ultimate form. Bearing in mind that fruiting shoots spring from the previous year's wood, it is possible that grapes could be formed as early as the second year. This is really too early because they will absorb energy which should be spent in extending the vine, and the bunches should be pinched out before flowering. From the third summer on fruit may be cropped though this should be limited to a few bunches until the vine reaches its ultimate size.

## The growing season

Although outdoor vines do not normally break bud until late April, those under glass may begin growth as much as two months earlier. Frosts are still a danger at this time of the year and care must be taken to close the house at night. Before the vines break dormancy, those trained in the vertical arm form should be untied from their wire and laid upon the floor of the house. If left upright the sap pressure will be greatest at the highest spurs resulting in uneven growth up the arm. As soon as the young shoots have emerged the arm may be retied to its wire. Care must be taken with this operation because the emerging shoots are very tender and can easily be snapped off. Horizontal arm-trained vines may be left in their permanent position because their spurs being at the same level will be subject to a more even sap pressure.

Just as growth may precede that of outdoor vines by up to two months, so may flowering. Successful flowering depends on satisfactory pollination and fertilisation which are encouraged by warmth and adequate (but not excessive) humidity. Damping down the house floor and careful attention to house ventilation should provide the ideal conditions. Many varieties, like most outdoor vines, are self-fertile, but some require pollinators. But self-fertile or not, the natural pollinating agent, wind, is seldom present in a house, and a little help with a soft brush or rabbit's tail in the same manner employed with peaches will ensure good fruitset. Once the berries have formed it is advisable to reduce the humidity in the house and increase the ventilation as much as possible on warm days, closing the house only at night or if the days are chilly.

Some varieties produce nice open clusters while others give a tighter bunch, but in either case if we wish to grow the largest, most attractive dessert grapes we must reduce the number of berries in each cluster. When winegrowing, the size of each individual berry is of no importance. The quality and quantity of juice is all that matters, and fifty small berries are as good as twenty large ones. However dessert grapes are undoubtedly more enjoyable if they are large. It is not possible to be specific as to how much you should thin the fruitlets. Often it is better to thin twice, once just after fruitset, and again about three weeks later, using pointed scissors. Fruitlets are removed evenly throughout the bunch so that the remainder have room to expand. If fruitset has been poor for some reason or other, a certain amount of natural thinning may have occurred so it is worth waiting to see that all the berries are swelling before reducing their number with scissors.

As the fruit develops, maintain a steady water supply by frequent, light watering so that there is adequate moisture for berry swelling. Infrequent heavy watering may result in the grapes splitting, and too little water will result in small fruit. When the grapes become attractive to wasps and birds the greenhouse has a tremendous advantage in that the doors and ventilators can be fitted with gauze screens to keep pests out. Screens should be just fine enough to prevent wasps' entry, but not so fine as to obstruct ventilation more than is absolutely necessary.

## Mildews

Vines under cover do not become saturated with rain or dew, but they receive far less ventilation than outdoor plants and mildew is therefore still a problem. House conditions most commonly favour oidium which is frequently seen on badly tended vines. Spraying is essential, the programme recommended for outdoor vines being adequate, though great care should be taken to avoid scorch caused by spraying in full sunlight, or at too great a concentration. Fungicides should be applied in the evening, the plant tissue being thoroughly covered in a fine mist, but not drenched.

# ℭℬ 10 The winery and cellar

Having decided on the grape varieties we are going to process into wine, the next step is to consider the premises and equipment necessary to do the job.

The country winemaker is usually very temperature conscious and tends to think in terms of cosy fermentation rooms and cupboards. It may therefore come as a pleasant surprise to learn that juice from the grape is not so demanding in this respect. The main reason for this is that wine yeasts and wine grapes are perfect partners. Centuries of selection, natural and otherwise, have resulted in strains of yeasts that find all they desire for active and reproductive life in winegrape juice. The addition of yeast nutrients to the must is normally quite unnecessary, and 'stuck' ferments should not occur. Should the weather be very cold at the time of starting a fermentation, a little artificial heat for a brief period may help the process to begin, but once it has, the need is more often to ensure the ferment is cool rather than warm.

This being so it is not necessary to go to enormous trouble and expense constructing specially insulated premises, even if you are making a hogshead of wine and have to work outside the house. By the time really heavy frosts occur, your grape juice should have turned into wine, and the average lightly built shed will give quite a lot of protection to vessels of wine. Due to the fact that alcohol will depress the freezing point of your wine, it would be necessary for the temperature to fall below −4°C before there is a chance of it freezing and rupturing the container. The air temperature would have to remain at this level for a considerable period to freeze any bulk of wine under cover. Should these conditions occur, a little artificial heat may be applied to the building, but paraffin heaters should only be used when the wine is in pore-free containers, as it will readily absorb the fumes with disastrous results!

The small-scale vintner working in the house need not fill up the shelves in the kitchen nor commandeer the airing cupboard. In fact such places are far too warm for fermentation, and an unheated spare bedroom or boxroom will be adequate. However, once your production reaches any size you may be forced outside. As the vinification is always carried on in the late autumn and winter months, some form of cover is essential, and naturally the larger your production, the larger your premises will have to be. If we consider the *most* the amateur is likely to need, the less ambitious will realise that they can get by with correspondingly less.

There *is* such a thing as a standard hogshead, but most nominal hogsheads vary from 200–300 litres (45–65 gallons) in capacity, therefore you may expect upwards of 300 bottles from most. This quantity is probably the maximum that most families would wish to make, and for the purposes of this book we will consider it the upper limit. The size of the cellar or winery needed to cope with this quantity will therefore be determined by the fact that it must be able to house at least two hogsheads, one full, the other for racking into. In addition, it will have to house an assortment of smaller containers for overspill, or for years when due to low yield less than a hogshead is made. Whether or not you crush and press the crop in your winery is up to you, but *some* working space is very important. There is nothing worse than doing ten rounds with a cask in a confined space!

A full hogshead will weigh in the region of 230kg (500lb) and it is vital to have a floor capable of taking the load. Equally important is a wide door through which at least empty barrels may be passed with ease. The cleaning and rinsing of casks is accomplished more easily in the open. A water hose is essential for this and other purposes, and it is a great advantage if the premises themselves can be washed down, although as long as they are kept clean this is not quite so important.

If you have the space, a work bench in a partitioned off clean area of the winery will be very handy for your 'lab' work, though this can easily be carried out elsewhere. Unless you have ample space to separate the two, great beefy barrels and delicate glass burettes do not mix very well.

## Winery equipment

The techniques of vinification will be descibed in Chapters 12 to 14, but I will try to describe a suitable range of equipment here.

The degree of sophistication of winery equipment will depend partly on the quantity of your production and partly on your inclination. The production of one or two gallons requires very little in the way of apparatus, but the work involved in vinting larger quantities will be very much reduced if certain items of equipment are acquired.

Acquisition can mean simply buying ready-made equipment, or manufacturing your own from whatever materials can be found. If you have anything of the beachcomber in you and you know where your local scrapyard is, it is amazing how often the right piece of material can be picked up for a few pence instead of paying pounds for it elsewhere or going without. A 'junkyard' mentality combined with the gentle art of 'instabodge' can do wonders. I should emphasise that by junkyard I mean general scrap merchants and not car breakers who usually have little of value to the winemaker. Most scrap merchants will let you rummage around their yard and take away whatever you find for the scrap value of the metal only.

### *Grape crushers*

One of the first processes necessary in converting grapes into wine is that of splitting the berry skins in order to release the juice. Whole grapes placed in a press will yield very little juice as they tend to cushion each other and are only burst with difficulty.

Grape crushing may, of course, be carried out without any equipment other than a large polythene bin or wooden tub and a pair of feet! The ancients, after all, crushed grapes by treading them, and a few people even today continue the tradition. There is nothing to stop you from treading your grapes, apart from the fact that the experience is not all it is cracked up to be this far north! In mid-October grape juice is *very* chilly and the operation is liable to cover you in a sticky coating of juice. Treading has survived so long in some cases because it is kind to the grapes and little damage is done to the stalks and pips. This is important because these parts contain high concentrations of substances such as tannin, which although important, should not feature too strongly in a wine.

If you do not feel up to treading your crop, and you have no great quantity, you may simply crush the bunches with your hands. A minor drawback to this method is that grape juice will be absorbed by your skin, where it will oxidise and stain your hands. If this worries you, the stains may be removed easily with lemon juice or citric acid solution. I would not recommend the use of either rubber gloves or barrier creams to prevent staining due to the likelihood of contaminating the juice.

Large crops will require some kind of mechanical crusher or mill. Suitable mills are now on the market, but they are not too difficult for the handyman to manufacture himself. A very adequate grapemill can be constructed from a few pieces of timber and a cannibalised mangle, always providing that you can find one in this day and age. Just such a mill made from a mangle is illustrated in Fig. 15. This apparatus has

**Figure 15** *Home-made grapemill.*

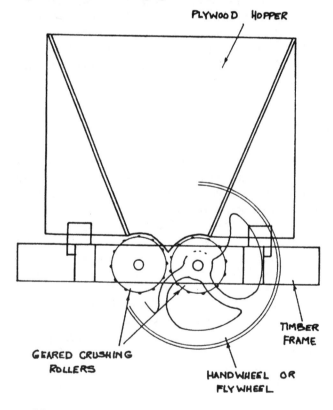

coped with quite large crops, but I know from unhappy experience that if you are making as much as a hogshead, some form of motorisation will add considerably to your life expectancy! This may be achieved by using a geared-down electric motor and flywheel.

It is necessary to stud or otherwise ridge the rollers in order that the slippery berries are caught and dragged through them. For this reason wooden rollers are preferable to the rubber type, apart from the fact that some grades of rubber will impart a taint to the juice. If mangle rollers cannot be found, it will be possible to purchase a pair of turned wooden rollers. They should be about 4 to 5 inches in diameter and not less than 12 inches long. They should be mounted so that they are separated by approximately one-eighth of an inch, partly to avoid the studs touching the opposite roller, but principally in order to let the stalks and pips pass through with as little damage as possible. Studs are best supplied in the form of round-headed, chrome-plated brass woodscrews, and they must be set so that those on one roller do not foul those on the other. Ideally, rollers should be geared together one end so that one is driven at a faster speed than the other. This will increase the tearing action on the berries. A simple varnished plywood hopper should be made to feed the bunches into the rollers.

## Grapepresses and alternatives

Growers of only one or two vines need have no mechanical press at all. I used to cope quite well with the crop from my few garden vines by literally wringing the juice from them. Wrap a few bunches at a time in a piece of synthetic netting and the bundle may be wrung out over a polythene bucket like a bit of washing. This method may sound crude, but unless you have a large quantity of fruit, it is effective and takes little time.

An alternative for very small crops is an electric juicer, although some tend to be rather rough with their contents. Also, unless they are going to be used for purposes other than just obtaining the juice from your grapes once a year, the expense would be better invested in a proper press.

There are several types of purpose-built presses on the market now, but to illustrate what can be made at very little expense from scrap materials, you should refer to Fig. 16. This small press was made, except

**Figure 16**   *Home-made grapepress.*

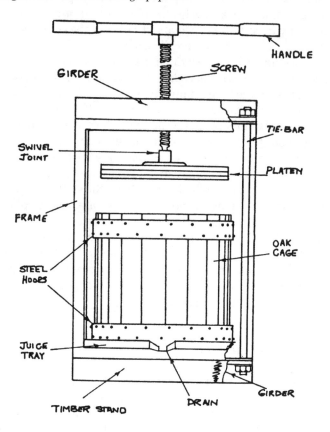

for the wood, entirely from scrapyard pickings. The frame was found already welded in that particular shape. The screw is a length of leadscrew from a lathe, and its nut is welded on to a simple piece of girder. Extra strength is lent to the frame by a similar piece of girder underneath, both being connected by a pair of long tie-bars. A pair of sturdy hoops for the cage and a length of bar for the screw handle complete the requirements. Total cost – under £2.00 at today's prices. The wood cost rather more but the whole press came to less than £20.00.

Such a press is ideal for most garden growers who are making a little more than just a few bottles, and the same basic design can be used to build larger presses for greater quantities. Naturally, if you are building a press from scrap parts, the design will vary from press to press. And it is little use being too specific here regarding measurements and details of construction, but some points are important.

Firstly, any non-stainless metal parts must be prevented from coming into contact with the juice by means of paint or varnish. The dangers of metal contamination will be discussed later, but it is a factor which must be considered with all equipment.

The cage should be built of oak if possible. The expense of the comparatively small quantity you will require will not be prohibitive, and its strength and durability are most desirable. The hoops should, of course, be painted before the staves are attached. The two are best joined by means of either chrome-plated brass screws, or more cheaply by japanned screws. The staves should be so arranged that the gap between them is about one-eighth of an inch. If it is much wider, the grape pulp in its net will try to escape between them! The completed cage should be quite rigid and removable from the press so that the pressed cake of skins and stalks may be extracted easily, and the cage cleaned.

The base tray may be constructed of two thicknesses of blockboard with a softwood rim, but it is a good idea to seal it well with poly-urethane varnish to ease cleaning and prevent de-lamination of the blockboard when wet. The platen may also be made of two thicknesses of blockboard, fitted with a steel load-spreading plate to take the screw. It is important that the press is so designed that it is either possible to remove the platen from the screw easily or to wind the platen up high enough to leave plenty of room for loading the cage with pulp.

Lubrication of the screw and any moving parts is best done with *Vaseline* which will not contaminate the juice. The usual mineral oils and greases should be avoided at all times.

An alternative press design which is easier to construct but more fiddly to use is shown in Fig. 17. Except for tiebolts it can be constructed entirely from wood, the mechanics being confined to a reasonably hefty car jack. The hand-wound type may be used but it is easier to employ a hydraulic type, which will generally also be more efficient. It is vital however, to ensure that hydraulic oil does not find its way into the juice. Commercial hydraulic grapepresses are constructed in such a way that the mechanics are beneath the cage, thus removing the danger of contamination.

*Figure 17* Utility grapepress using hydraulic jack.

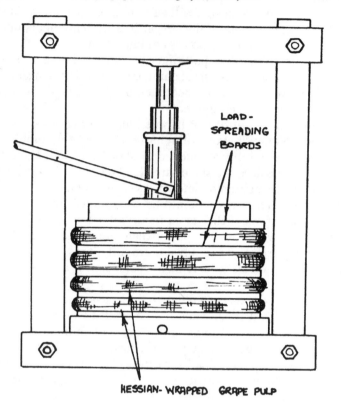

LOAD-
SPREADING
BOARDS

HESSIAN- WRAPPED GRAPE PULP

## Fermentation vessels

### Small containers

You will probably be familiar with the use of glass carboys, which vary
in capacity from 2 to 50 litres (half to ten gallons) or more. For small
volumes of wine there is really nothing better. They are particularly
attractive to the novice because their transparency allows the vintner
to see what is going on inside, but above all they are easy to clean and
maintain. Although plastics are replacing them, glass carboys are still
fairly easy to obtain.

Polythene is an extremely useful material for miscellaneous pieces of equipment such as buckets and funnels, but some care must be taken when fermenting in polythene. Certain grades are prone to pick up taints and pass them on. Glass may be more vulnerable to damage but in most other respects it is a preferable material.

Even if you are making a hogshead, you will need a range of smaller vessels. This range should be so designed that the contents of any single vessel may be accommodated in a number of smaller vessels. Unless you are desperate, the very convenient country winemaking practice of topping up with water after racking is not employed. This means that a little will be lost from the total volume at each racking, and the racked quantity must be held in one or more smaller vessels to avoid excessive contact with the air, unless topping-up wine is available.

## Casks

Quantities much in excess of 45 litres (ten gallons) can either be contained in a series of large carboys, or more practically in a cask. Inexpensive once-used chestnut wine barrels may be obtained from several of the importing winehouses. Although oak barrels can be purchased at extra expense, chestnut is adequate unless you wish to store your wine in cask for a considerable period. Normally northern white wines are best transferred from the wood to the bottle as soon as they are ready. Carefully maintained, casks will last for years, but careless treatment will soon render them useless.

Barrels from different regions tend to vary a little, but their basic construction is the same. They are designed for ease of movement and maximum strength. A typical hogshead is illustrated in Fig. 18.

If you obtain casks from a wine importer, you should tell him what they are to be used for and he will probably go to the trouble of selecting particularly suitable barrels. If you are going to make white wine, you should specify ex-white casks, because those which have previously held red wine will tint the next occupant accordingly. Even if this has little effect on the taste, the appearance will be spoiled. Ex-beer barrels are best avoided all together, as taint is inevitable in the wine.

*Figure 18*  *Wooden cask.*

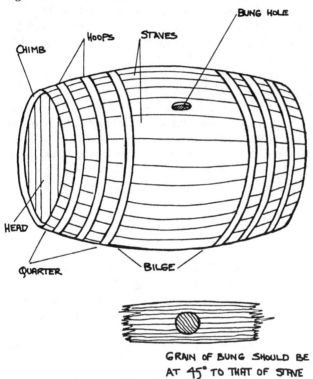

GRAIN OF BUNG SHOULD BE
AT 45° TO THAT OF STAVE

## Cask bungs

Extracting the bung from a barrel may appear to be a bit of a problem at first, but there is a simple method of extracting it without damage. Using a wooden or rubber mallet (a metal hammer will damage the staves), strike the bung stave smartly either side of the bung a few times. A few blows should cause the bung to pop out easily. Nothing else should be necessary unless the bung has been hammered home wrongly. Bungs should be undersize for their hole, and made to fit snugly by one or two thicknesses of clean hessian. When knocked home, their grain should run at 45° to that of the bung stave as shown in Fig. 18.

## Cask maintenance and storage

Your barrels will probably have been sulphured before arrival, so do *not* remove the bung and eagerly take a great lungful of the contents! Sniff it carefully. If, apart from the pungent smell of sulphur dioxide gas, your barrel smells sweet and is clean, it will only be necessary to fill it with clean water sulphited at a rate of 500mg $SO_2$/litre, or approximately 220g (8oz) sodium metabisulphite per 50 gallons of water. To aid the release of sulphur dioxide gas, about 50g (2oz) citric acid should be added at the same time to acidify the barrel contents slightly.

Using these quantities of sodium metabisulphite, it is obviously best to buy it in bulk, and 1kg and 3kg packs can be purchased inexpensively (see Appendix A). It should be stored in a sealed container – preferably of glass.

Before filling a cask with water, or anything else for that matter, it must be chocked up, level, bung uppermost and clear of the ground. Four wooden chocks should be placed as shown in Fig. 19, beneath the

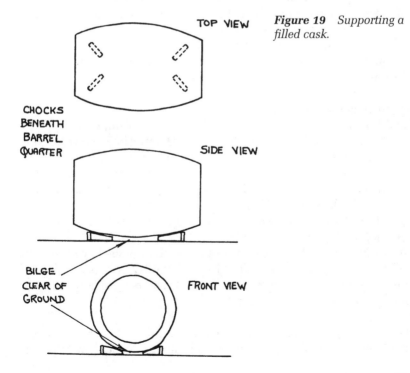

**Figure 19**  *Supporting a filled cask.*

TOP VIEW

CHOCKS BENEATH BARREL QUARTER

SIDE VIEW

BILGE CLEAR OF GROUND

FRONT VIEW

quarters of the cask. This will spread the load on four strong points instead of bearing on one stave at the bilge. A full hogshead weighs about a quarter of a ton, and this mass bearing on one point for any length of time will strain that stave, causing it to spring.

Chocks may be sawn from a piece of 4 × 2 timber and should be cut at such an angle that they fit the contour of the cask as snugly as possible. The position of the hoops should also be checked before filling. Their chief function is to hold the staves together – if they are loose the barrel will leak. Loose hoops should be knocked towards the bilge using a hammer and drift to avoid undue damage to the staves.

Barrels must never be left empty for any great length of time or the staves will dry out and shrink so that the barrel springs badly. Should this occur you may be able to salvage the barrel by leaving a hose running into it until it swells and takes up, but the occasion should never be allowed to arise.

Casks that are to be used soon after arrival need not be filled with sulphite solution, but may be kept sweet by burning a sulphur taper (see Appendix A), on a length of wire inside the loosely bunged barrel. The wire and taper is then removed and the barrel is bunged normally. Whether your barrel has been filled with water or merely had a taper burned in it, it must be well rinsed with clean water immediately before use.

**Cask inspection and cleaning**
Visual inspection of the inside of a cask is almost impossible with a torch. There is simply not enough room at the bung hole for a torch *and* an eye. A simple but very efficient lamp can be made using a plain 40 watt candle bulb and bulb holder on a length of plastic-covered flex. The bulb can be lowered into the cask, and the holder will shield your eyes from the direct glare. The whole interior will be well illuminated and at least the bottom half, which is the most likely half to need inspection, will be clearly visible.

Apart from any whiff of sulphur dioxide, should one of your barrels smell not quite sweet, or should it be visibly dirty, it must be cleaned perfectly before use. Well maintained barrels will not need special treatment, but foul casks may be dealt with as follows.

**General dirt** – grime is best removed by mechanical means. Put into the cask either a clean piece of chain or some stones, together with two or three gallons of water, then rumble the cask around for a while so that the inside receives a good scouring. Remove the stones or chain, rinse well and inspect. Repeat the action if required.

**Acetification** – casks smelling of vinegar *must* be treated chemically or taint will ruin the wine if infection does not. The barrel should first be filled with clean water and left to stand for two days. It should then be emptied and have 120g (4oz) sodium hydroxide added (take care – *caustic*), together with about two gallons of boiling water. Sodium hydroxide and water react together to produce heat. This reaction can be violent, especially if the water is boiling, so pour the hydroxide crystals into the cask first, then add the boiling water through a funnel. Never try mixing the two outside the cask or you could be showered with boiling caustic solution! This solution is left inside for twelve hours, the cask being rolled around every two hours to rinse the whole interior thoroughly. It is important not to forget the heads of the cask during this operation. Finally the barrel should be rinsed with clean water several times, and then filled with sodium metabisulphite solution as described earlier.

**Mustiness** – this can usually be removed by rinsing the barrel with a solution of 20g (¾oz) calcium chloride dissolved in a gallon of water for two hours, followed by a good rinsing with clean water.

Needless to say, casks which refuse to respond to treatment and persist in smelling in the least foul, are best cut in half and used as flower tubs! Certainly they should never be used for wine.

### Cask capacity

It is very important to have a good idea of the capacity of a barrel when making additions of sugar, finings or any other material at a specific rate. As casks vary in size somewhat, and their volume is not always inscribed on their head, it is useful to know how to calculate the volume of a cask with a reasonable degree of accuracy. This can be done by taking three measurements as shown in Fig. 20, followed by a simple calculation.

If A is the diameter of the head in inches, B the distance between the heads and C the internal diameter at the bung, the capacity of the cask in gallons is given overleaf (Fig. 20).

**Figure 20**   *Cask volume estimation.*

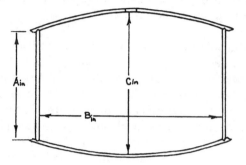

$$0.000944 \times B(2C^2 + A^2)$$

(to convert to litres multiply by 4.546)

Measurement of the head diameter is easy enough, and so too is the internal diameter at the bung. The separation between the two heads is a little more difficult, and you must not forget to allow for the thickness of the head staves, which may be taken as approximately one inch each end.

A more accurate but more tedious method of measurement is to fill the cask using a smaller container of known capacity, as many times as is required.

## Vats

The fermentation of red and rosé wine is started on the whole pulp. Open but loosely lidded containers must therefore be used at this stage. These are easy to come by, and depending on the volume of your pulp, you may use polythene buckets or bins, or casks that have been sawn in half. Half casks must be maintained in the same way as whole casks and should never be allowed to dry out, nor their contents to become stagnant.

## Fermentation locks

Those who have no previous winemaking experience will be unfamiliar with the use of fermentation locks. Quite simply, these allow the escape of carbon dioxide evolved during fermentation without allowing the entry of undesirable organisms. Locks vary in design, but perhaps the most popular, and certainly that most used by commercial vintners, is the polystyrene type shown in Fig. 21. The lock is set in a bored bung of cork or tasteless rubber, of such a diameter that it snugly fits the neck of your carboy or bung hole of your cask. It is filled to the level indicated with water containing a little sodium metabisulphite.

**Figure 21**   *Fermentation lock.*

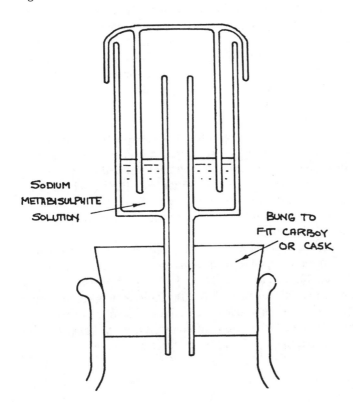

SoDIUM
METABISULPHITE
SOLUTION

BUNG TO
FIT CARBOY
OR CASK

Gas escaping from the ferment bubbles through the lock, as must any air movement in the opposite direction. The solution in the lock ensures sterilisation of bacteria or yeasts in that air. The solution will lose its effectiveness after a month, and it should be renewed regularly after this period.

Locks come in several sizes. The larger the fermenting bulk, the larger should be the lock. If it is too small there is the danger that the carbon dioxide will not be able to escape freely, and the lock contents may be emptied or the lock may be blown off bodily! A 25mm (1in.) diameter lock will generally be sufficient for a 5-litre (one-gallon) carboy, but hogsheads should not be fitted with locks smaller than 75mm (3in.) outside diameter.

The volume of carbon dioxide produced during fermentation is quite considerable, and while we are discussing winery equipment, it is worth considering ventilation. This is not of more than passing interest to the maker of one or two gallons (5-10l), but a hogshead of grape must will evolve about 9000 litres of carbon dioxide during the ferment. Naturally this does not come off all at once, the bulk of it evolving over a period of one to two weeks. In a ventilated room or in an outside shed this gas will quickly dissipate, but lest you decide to use a small underground cellar for a winery, I feel bound to express a word of caution.

In a poorly ventilated winery, carbon dioxide, being heavier than air, will lie in an ever-deepening layer near the floor. The depth of this layer will obviously depend on the size of the room and the bulk of the ferment, but a small space, say eight feet square, containing a hogshead, could become filled with carbon dioxide to a depth of 1.5m. Few are likely to experience these conditions, but should they occur, there is a very real danger of asphyxiation!

Those who suspect there is any risk may borrow a safety trick that commercial vintners use. Some of the larger English vineyards may have more than 20,000 litres of must fermenting, and the daily output of carbon dioxide may peak at 100,000 litres. Under these conditions, vintners use lighted candles as carbon dioxide indicators when working in their cellars. The candles are snuffed out if the level of gas in the cellar rises too high, and the winery is speedily evacuated!

## Siphons and stackpipes

Small quantities of juice or wine may be racked from one vessel to another by means of a simple length of polythene tube used as a siphon. Slightly more sophisticated self-priming siphons may be purchased and these are much easier to use.

Racking from a large vessel or cask requires a stackpipe which may be lowered into the vessel, and reach the bottom if required. These may be made from stainless steel or one of several rigid plastics. The lower end of the pipe must be modified in order to avoid sucking up lees unless required in operations such as cleaning. Fig. 22 shows a simple modification enabling a pipe to be used for either drawing off clear must or wine, or for sucking the lees from the bottom.

**Figure 22**   *Simple variable stackpipe.*

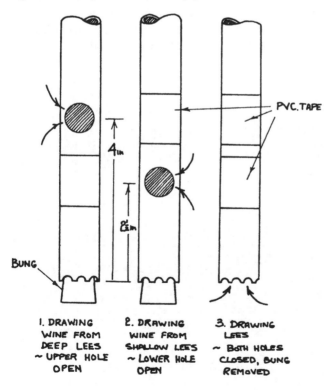

105 ∞

A length of approximately 20mm bore ABS cistern overflow pipe is cut to such a length that it will comfortably reach the bilge of your cask, leaving a few inches outside the bung hole. To this is attached a length of flexible polythene tube, either for use as a siphon or to lead to a pump. A series of notches are filed into the circumference of the lower end of the pipe, so that when sucking out dregs, the suction does not draw the pipe to the bottom, causing an interruption of flow. Two 12–15mm diameter holes are made in the side of the pipe, one at about 60mm, and the other at about 100mm from the end. Experience will teach you the ideal position of these holes for your own particular circumstances.

When racking off from a vessel with a deep layer of lees, a cork is inserted in the end of the pipe and the lower hole is sealed with PVC adhesive tape (momentary contact with this material is harmless). When racking from a vessel with a firm lees, the lower hole is uncovered while the upper is sealed. To suck up the lees, both holes are sealed and the cork is removed. It is simple but effective.

Apparatus for the measurement and treatment of juice and wine will be described as we come to each process in turn, and special equipment used in connection with sparkling wines will be discussed in Chapter 16.

# ය 11 The vintage

The practical business of winemaking begins with the gathering of the crop, and in England this normally takes place around mid-October.

*34. Harvesting Mueller-Thurgau grapes in early October.*

For the commercial grower, the exact date will depend on various factors such as the variety or varieties being grown, the quality of the past season, the availability of pickers and the weather around vintage time. Cropping at a rate of 3–5 tons per acre (7–12 tonnes per hectare), the commercial vintage requires considerable organisation if the fruit is to be gathered in good weather conditions and at optimum ripeness, and inevitably luck plays a role.

Garden growers have a great advantage in that the size of their crop will enable the harvest to be completed in a short time. If only a few kilos of grapes are to be gathered, you may risk waiting for the ideal moment with less of an eye on weather tendencies. The crop for 10 litres of wine is only 14kg and it may be picked in fifteen minutes. The hogs-head producer, on the other hand, will have a crop of 400kg which may involve two man-days' picking.

## Ripeness

Unfortunately it is not possible to measure the degree of ripeness of your grapes by taste. Each variety has its own acid to sugar ratio at different stages of ripeness, and though your tongue may try to tell you that one grape has more sugar than another, the reverse may well be true.

This can be illustrated by the two very popular varieties, Mueller-Thurgau with a low acid value, and Seyval Blanc with a relatively high acid value. If the berries of one are tasted against the other when, shall we say, the sugar of both is at 19%, the Mueller-Thurgau fruit will taste sweeter.

I should emphasise that acidity is very important and if you judge your crop maturity by sugar alone, you may grow over-ripe grapes yielding a lifeless wine. With some experience of your own varieties you should be able to get *some* idea of ripeness, but you will not be able to guess the gravity very accurately.

In most reasonable sites in southern England, the quality varieties mentioned in this book, that is the non-vigorous varieties, will be ripe enough to pick from mid-October on. If you have no other means of measuring the ripeness of your crop this will be a fair guide, although early varieties such as Madeleine Sylvaner or Siegerrebe will sometimes be ready in mid-September. Remember that our October weather is often warm enough to push quite a lot more sugar into the fruit, and a few extra good days may be particularly beneficial after a poor summer.

The ideal gravities to aim for are mentioned in Chapter 3 and those who wish to know the maturity of their crop with any degree of accuracy must use one of two methods of measurement. You may not be familiar with them so I offer a brief description of them here.

## The hydrometer

Although cheap and simple, this instrument is wasteful with juice, and so it is not much use as a ripening progress watcher to the grower of two or three vines. Nevertheless, the hydrometer will *have* to be used after the harvest anyway, and so it is appropriate to describe it here.

Various makes of the instrument, shown typically in Fig. 23, are readily available (see Appendix A). Its purpose is to show the specific gravity of a liquid and it is calibrated to work within a certain range. The specific gravity of a liquid is the ratio of its own mass compared to that of the same volume of water at a certain temperature. This may sound complicated, but put more simply, a liquid with a specific gravity of 1.080 is 1.080 times heavier than the same volume of water. Similarly, a liquid with a specific gravity of 0.995 has only 0.995 of the mass of an equal volume of water.

Grape juice is heavier than water, mainly due to the heavier-than-water sugar content, but to a much lesser degree to other compounds also. The highest gravities likely to be encountered in winemaking will be with dessert wine musts which may start around 1.120, or exceptionally at 1.140. The lowest gravity after fermentation will be in the region of 0.990. You should, therefore, obtain a hydrometer with a calibrated range of 0.990–1.140. This will serve as a general-purpose instrument. You may also, if you wish, purchase narrow range instruments for greater accuracy but they are generally not necessary.

In vinification we tend to speak not of specific gravities, but of degrees Oechsle or °Oe. This scale, as mentioned earlier, is simply the specific gravity less the unit and decimal point. Hence a specific gravity of 1.073 is 73°Oe and a specific gravity of 1.113 is 113°Oe.

As the hydrometer has to be floated in the liquid being measured, you must naturally have a container to hold the juice, and glass cylinders can be purchased with your hydrometer. The cylinder is filled with

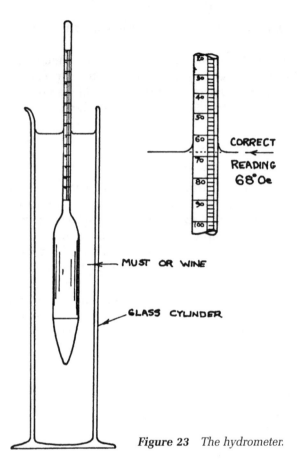

**Figure 23**   *The hydrometer.*

enough grape juice to float the hydrometer which is lowered gently into the liquid, bulb downwards. Care should be taken to spin off any bubbles which attach themselves to the instrument or they will falsify the reading. When the hydrometer has had a chance to come to rest at its natural depth, the calibrated stem will be cut at a certain point by the surface of the liquid. Due to surface tension, the liquid will form a curved meniscus with the stem, and the correct gravity is read from the scale at the level of the *bottom of* the meniscus, as shown in Fig. 23. Do not forget that the value of the scale increases from top to bottom. The reading shown therefore is 1.068, not 1.072.

When measuring freshly pressed grape juice, two correction factors may have to be applied. Firstly, the juice will contain millions of tiny suspended pulp particles, and these being heavier than the juice will elevate the gravity reading – 0.002 or 2°Oe should be subtracted from the reading to allow for this effect.

Secondly, the density of a liquid is affected by its temperature. The colder it is, the more dense it will be and vice versa. Most hydrometers are calibrated to read accurately at 20°C. Generally, grape juice in mid-October will be nearer 10°C, therefore the juice must either be warmed to 20°C before measuring the specific gravity, or alternatively a correction must be made. The correction factor varies a little according to the temperature range concerned, but for our purposes it is sufficiently accurate to say that for every 5°C below the hydrometer calibration temperature, you should subtract 1°Oe from your hydrometer reading.

To clarify this let us consider an example. Some grapes are pressed and the juice is collected in the test cylinder. The hydrometer is floated in the juice, and when steady, the bottom of the meniscus is level with the mark denoting a gravity of 1.073 on the scale. The temperature of the juice is found by thermometer to be 10°C. The correct reading should therefore be 73°Oe, less 2° for suspended pulp, less 2° for temperature or 73° – 2° – 2°=69°Oe.

Naturally if a hydrometer is used to measure the ripeness of your crop, a truly representative cross section of the crop must be taken. It is no use just picking out the ripest bunches.

## The refractometer

Ironically, although this instrument is capable of giving a very good idea of crop ripeness at the cost of only a few berries, and would therefore be well suited to the small grower, its own cost puts it beyond the pocket of most amateurs. Few people will feel inclined to spend £60.00 on a refractometer if they have only one or two vines. Nevertheless, these instruments are used in many fields these days, and you may have access to one even if you cannot buy one. There are different types of refractometer however, and any used for vinting must be calibrated for sugar solution and nothing else. The hogshead producer may feel he can justify the expense of an instrument as he will be making so much inexpensive wine.

The instrument is illustrated in Fig. 24. While the hydrometer relies on the Archimedes principle, the refractometer relies on the fact that the density of a medium affects its refractive index. In plain English this means that a light ray passing from one medium to another (unless at right-angles), such as from glass to water, will be bent. If that ray passes from glass to sugar solution, it will be bent *more*. Hence by passing a light ray through grape juice held between glass, the degree by which the ray is deflected will indicate the concentration of the sugar in the juice.

In practice the method is simplicity itself. A flap is opened at one end of the instrument, exposing two glass faces, which are in fact prisms. A grape berry is squeezed to deposit a drop of juice on one face, and the flap is closed, trapping a film of juice between the prisms. The refractometer is then held up to the light, and by looking through the eyepiece, a scale will be seen across the field of view. This scale, usually calibrated in percent sugar, will be cut by a shadow at a point depending on the sugar content of that berry. Thus a direct reading may be taken in a few seconds, although like the hydrometer, the instrument will have been

**Figure 24**   *The refractometer.*

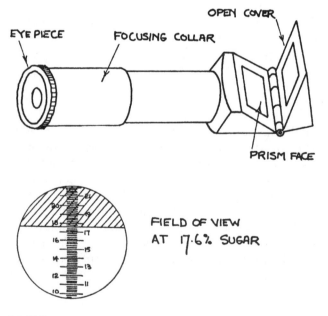

*35. Reading a refractometer
to obtain the sugar content of
grape juice.*

calibrated for a certain temperature, and the appropriate correction will
have to be made from the table supplied with the instrument. Of course,
you have only measured the ripeness of one berry, and it is necessary
to take several berries from several bunches to obtain a good average
crop ripeness.

## Picking

Unless it is unavoidable, you should pick your crop on a dry day.
Harvesting in the rain or from wet vines is not only very uncomfortable
but also causes dilution of the juice. Wine-grape bunches, not being
thinned, are usually quite tight and they will hold a lot of rainwater
between the berries. It is rather annoying to grow a crop to a gravity of
70°0e only to have it watered down to 60°Oe by rain.

The best tools for cutting the fruit from the vines are purpose-made
grape shears (see Appendix A). These come in two common types – one
like a cross between tin snips and pinking scissors, and the other like

a cross between secateurs and scissors. Both types can give you a nasty nip but it would take a degree of effort to cut a fingertip off. Secateurs however can manage such a minor operation effortlessly, and they should be avoided at harvest time. This may sound over-cautious, but when picking you quickly become careless. As you usually hold a bunch with the left hand while cutting with the right, the former is very vulnerable, especially as you often work by feel alone due to foliage and grapes obscuring the line of sight.

If we ever had traditional gathering hods in England, they have long since been forgotten, and standard polythene buckets are used widely, even in large vineyards. They have the advantage of being light, easy to clean and leakproof. The last point is important as grapes are often damaged during picking and no precious juice must be lost. On occa-

*36. Pruning secateurs which should not be used for harvesting, and cutters which are much safer.*

sions, grape bunches become so grown around wires that they can only be picked by holding the bucket beneath while cutting the bunch to pieces. At the end of the day any gathering equipment should be thoroughly cleaned to prevent contamination of the following day's crop with oxidised juice.

Large crops may be stored for processing in polythene bins, but only for one or two hours or spoilage will take place. It is vital that no grapes are picked that cannot be dealt with on the same day, and as soon as possible the harvested fruit should be taken to the winery for milling, pressing and sulphiting. Untreated bins left standing around overnight run the risk of oxidation and wild yeast ferments, both of which will spoil the wine.

# cଷ 12 Preparation of the must

Much of the next three chapters applies to all types of wine, but they are specifically devoted to still table wines. The special aspects of sparkling and dessert wines are dealt with in Chapter 16.

So far our progress towards wine has been limited to collecting the raw material, and some knowledge of what this consists of will help us understand the reasons for various vinting techniques. Fig. 25 illustrates a typical wine grape.

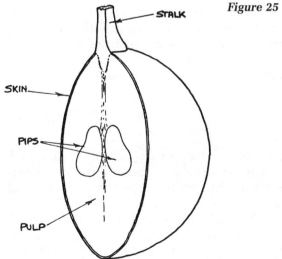

**Figure 25**   *The grape berry.*

Each berry is neatly packaged in its own skin, the function of which is mainly protective. It is the skin's thickness only which separates the fermentable juice from the yeasts in the bloom. Like most living matter the skin is composed mainly of water, but it contains up to 2% tannin, and, more importantly in black grapes, it holds the red anthocyanin pigment.

The pulp forms the bulk of the berry, accounting for 80–85% of its weight. It is in turn 75–80% water, 10–25% sugar and up to 6% other constituents such as acids, proteins and mineral salts. The sugar stored in the berries, which is in fact manufactured in the leaves by means of photosynthesis, is in the form of glucose and fructose in roughly equal proportion.

The acids in a grape are vital. They are essential requirements for active yeasts and give the finished wine life and freshness, as well as good keeping properties. Grape acids are mainly in the form of tartaric, malic and to a lesser extent citric acids. The further a grape progresses towards maturity, the less malic and more tartaric acid it will contain.

Pips and stalks are important only in as much as their constituents are best kept out of the wine as much as possible and this is achieved by careful handling. The pips especially contain high levels of tannin and oils, both of which will lead to harshness if they feature too strongly in the end product.

A certain degree of tannin is desirable in wine but this is normally supplied by the skins and stalks during normal processing. Red wines need more tannin than white wines, which is fortunate as prolonged contact with the skins is necessary for the extraction of colour. Nevertheless, excessive tannin can still pose problems here and for this reason red berries are usually stripped from the stalks before milling.

## Yeasts

The miracle agency by which our grape juice is converted into wine is the lowly yeast. There are in fact many thousands of different yeasts in nature. With every breath we draw yeasts into our lungs, for they are everywhere about us.

Unfortunately most of them are what we term wild yeasts, capable of producing only poor or even sick wine. Kloeckera and pichia for example, shown in Fig. 26, are quite unsuitable for the production of

**Figure 26**   *Yeasts.*

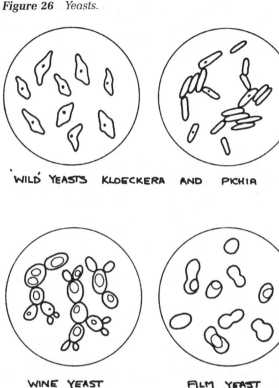

WILD YEASTS   KLOECKERA   AND   PICHIA

WINE YEAST
SACCHAROMYCES
CERIVISIAE

FILM YEAST
(NOT FLOR)
CANDIDA

high quality wine. Not only do they have a low alcohol tolerance, resulting in their death when they have produced as little as 5 ot 6% alcohol, but they also need oxygen which is quickly exhausted by sulphur
dioxide additions and displaced by carbon dioxide produced in the
ferment.

The most widely used wine yeasts belong to the saccharomyces
group, particularly S. cerevisiae, also illustrated in Fig. 26. Among the
advantages of the best strains of this yeast are that they have high alcohol tolerance, they work at low temperatures, they settle out quickly
after fermentation and they form a firm lees unlikely to be stirred up
during racking procedures.

It is our misfortune in northern Europe that the cooler the climate, the poorer the quality of the natural yeast in the bloom of the grape unless the vineyard is well established. After many years a natural high quality yeast population will inhabit the soil, but until then selected cultures are preferable.

## Starters

In order to have an active culture of an appropriate yeast ready when required, you should prepare a starter, two or three days before you plan to harvest your crop. Many suitable yeast cultures are now available to the amateur (see Appendix A). Prepare your starter according to the supplied recommended culture instructions but using grape juice as the medium. This should previously have been pressed from a few bunches of your crop and pasteurised by keeping it at 85°C for 30 minutes, and then cooled in a container plugged with cotton wool.

It is foolish to use anything but the most appropriate type of yeast, and general-purpose wine yeast should be avoided. If you are making a white wine use a Mosel-type, and if you are making a red or rosé use a Burgundy-type. It is worth going to the trouble of using liquid cultures as they are generally 100% what they claim to be – dried cultures tend to be contaminated with other strains. The commercial vineyards in England use cultures supplied by the German wine institutes, and some good yeasts are available to the amateur (see Appendix A).

## Records

From the moment the fruit arrives at the winery, it is important to keep a record of as many facts as possible. In this way you will be able to modify your process in future years if necessary, while having recorded facts on which to base your modifications. Similarly the causes of any faults which occur may be traced by reference to your log, and it can act as an excellent check list of vital operations. The progress of your wine should be logged from milling to bottling.

## Must destined for white table wine

White wine, as we have seen earlier, can be made from either white or black grapes, and both are handled identically for this purpose, but remember that some hybrids have pink juice.

The fruit is first fed through a mill, trodden or crushed by hand as described in Chapter 10. The skins having been split, the pulp may be collected in a container such as a polythene bin. Lidded dustbins are ideal for large quantities, and smaller bins of similar design are available for small crops. Do *not* use PVC bins.

The pulp should be left standing around for as little time as possible, and may be passed to the press straight away. If there is an unavoidable hold-up and crushed fruit has to be left unpressed overnight, it is essential to sulphite it at a rate of approximately 1–2g sodium metabisulphite per gallon (0.2–0. 5g/1) of pulp.

## Pressing

The techniques of pressing small quantities of fruit have already been described. Those who have a large crop to deal with however, and have a proper press, will find the following techniques will ease the process considerably.

White grapes, and black grapes destined for white wine, may be left on the stalk during pressing. Commercial machinery removes the stalks during milling, but they can provide drainage channels through the press-cake and also stabilise the slippery mass of berries in the cage.

It is important that the grape pulp is held in a net of 3–6mm (⅛–¼in.) mesh. This is to ensure that the pulp is retained in the press and not extruded between the staves, as it almost certainly will be if not restrained. Fresh grape pulp is extremely slippery and if placed in the cage alone, it will be quite unhandleable.

Do not try to rush the process or you will strain both the press and yourself, and you will obtain less juice more slowly. To start with much of the juice will pass straight through the press without any pressure at all. This is the 'free run' juice and is normally of the highest quality. On applying pressure the juice will run fast to begin with, but will gradually slow down. Do not screw the platen down too hard too quickly. When it becomes stiff to turn leave it for a while and let the pressure dissipate, then apply a little more pressure and wait again. When you feel you are nearing the end of that pressing, it is a good plan to ease the screw back a few turns every now and again to let the drainage channels open up again. Reapplication of the pressure will then result in better juice expression.

Do not risk a rupture trying to press the pulp to tinder dryness. The law of diminishing returns will ensure that the longer you press, the less will be your reward per minute. Also the tail of the pressing will be lower in quality than the rest and so it is less important, and really hard pressing will also risk releasing excess tannin and other undesirables from the pips and stalks. Another hazard of extended pressing is that juice which spends a long time coming from the press is all the while oxidising and will spoil the bulk.

When the pulp has had a good pressing, remove it from the cage, break up the cake, and return it for a second pressing. It is surprising how much more juice will be extracted from material which seemed all but dry after the first pressing. The procedure should not be repeated further however, or you will risk the spoilage problems I have just mentioned.

It is vital that the press and all other equipment is cleaned down at the end of the day so that no juice is left around to oxidise and contaminate the following day's pressing.

The juice running from the press will not be crystal clear as it contains millions of suspended pulp particles, dust and other solid bodies. For the highest quality wine it is necessary to let these suspended bodies settle out before proceeding with the ferment. However, even before settling is allowed to proceed, there are one or two jobs to be done.

## Must preservation

First and foremost the juice must be prevented from undergoing any form of spoilage. As soon as each batch of grapes has been pressed, the resulting juice must be collected in a covered or closed vessel, and sulphited at a rate of approximately 120mg $SO_2$/litre of must. In practice this works out sufficiently closely to an addition of 1g sodium metabisulphite per gallon of juice. (I make no apology for mixing imperial and metric measurements here, as many of you will be dealing with carboys with the known capacity measured in gallons, and it is easier to speak of a gram than ½₈ of an ounce!)

The weighing of small quantities requires a balance. It does not need to be super-accurate and a very adequate instrument can be bought for a few pounds (see Appendix A). Not everyone will wish to go to this expense however, even though the balance may often be required during the vinification. The only alternative is to prevail upon the services of the local dispensary, or in this particular case, for small quantities of juice, Campden tablets may be used. One tablet, which is best crushed between two spoons before use, contains the approximate equivalent of 0.5g sodium metabisulphite.

The correct quantity of powder is dissolved in a small quantity of juice and this is then stirred into the bulk.

If you do not have the facilities for accuracy with this sulphite dose, it is better to err slightly on the heavy side. Under-sulphiting may be insufficient to protect the juice, but overdoses, unless excessive, may be corrected. The main reasons for sulphiting are the prevention of oxidation, leading to loss of freshness, and to kill harmful bacteria and wild yeasts which are likely to start undesirable ferments. Once the procedure has been carried out correctly, and the juice is held in a sealed container with little air space, it will keep safely for a considerable period.

Although now safe, the juice is not yet allowed to stand for settling. You must first measure its acidity and its sugar content and adjust these if necessary.

## Must sugar content

Grape juice grown in northern Europe frequently needs a small addition of sugar to boost the potential alcohol to a level that will assure good keeping qualities in the finished wine. Do not run away with the idea that it is only in England that this sugaring of the must, or chaptalisation, is sometimes necessary. Most German table wines, as well as some from the Loire and Burgundy, are produced from chaptalised musts in the average year.

In some years chaptalisation will not be required and, as we have seen before, the garden grower is less likely to need to chaptalise than the large vineyard owner. If you are growing the correct varieties on a suitable site, sugaring, even when necessary, should seldom amount to more than 2–3oz per gallon of juice – a far cry from most country wine requirements.

We have already discussed the measurement of juice sugar content by means of a hydrometer in the last chapter, but whether you used the method during the ripening period or not, you *must* do so now. Adjustment to the desired gravity may easily be calculated by reference to the table below. The lowest allowable natural gravity before chaptalisation in commercial growing is about 50°Oe. This limit is usually easily surpassed by 20° or so but it has been established because no matter how much sugar is loaded into really unripe juice, only very poor wine will result. The ripening of the grape is a complex process, concerned not only with sugar and acid, but with other vital constituents also. For this reason you should discard any varieties which consistently fail to produce reasonably high gravities.

The ideal gravity for must that is to be made into English wine is between 80° and 85°Oe, after chaptalisation. This will result in an alcohol content of around 11%. Do not be tempted to chaptalise to a higher gravity as too high an alcohol content will be incompatible with the character of an English wine and destroy its delicacy. We are trying to make a fine wine, not rocket fuel.

The necessary sugar addition, if required, is calculated from the table. Plain white sugar is easiest to use, and is stirred into the juice until dissolved. This sugar is not in a readily fermentable form, but the yeast will soon invert it naturally.

**Adjustment of juice sugar content**

| Natural juice gravity | °Oe | Potential alcohol % by volume | Amount of sugar to add to each gallon to bring the gravity to 82°Oe | |
|---|---|---|---|---|
| 1.050 | 50 | 6.5 | 13oz | (370g) |
| 1.055 | 55 | 7.2 | 11oz | (310g) |
| 1.060 | 60 | 7.8 | 9oz | (255g) |
| 1.065 | 65 | 8.6 | 7oz | (200g) |
| 1.070 | 70 | 9.2 | 5oz | (140g) |
| 1.075 | 75 | 9.9 | 3oz | (85g) |
| 1.080 | 80 | 10.6 | 1oz | (30g) |
| 1.082 | 82 | 11.0 | 0 | |

## Must acidity

Most varieties grown in suitable areas will not produce crops with over-acid juice in the average year, and indeed a reasonable level of acid is essential as we have seen. Nevertheless it is necessary to measure the acidity of the must and make adjustments if required.

Although certain varieties can be a little low in acid value if left on the vine too long, the level can be raised by the calculated addition of tartaric acid. In very poor summers other varieties may produce juice with too much acid, and this must be reduced.

Acidity measurement is achieved by a simple method called 'titration'. The necessary materials and apparatus are inexpensive, and a supplier is listed in Appendix A.

| Apparatus required (see Fig. 27) | Chemicals required |
|---|---|
| 1 × 5ml pipette | N/10 (decinormal) sodium hydroxide |
| 1 × 25ml graduated burette and stand | Distilled water |
| 1 × 250ml conical flask | 1% phenolphthalein |

**Method**

First rinse the 5ml pipette with some of the juice, then draw juice up into the pipette past the graduation mark by sucking. Try to avoid the temptation of guzzling juice and remember it is potential wine! Quickly place your fingertip over the top end to prevent the juice running straight out, and then by easing the finger up let the juice drop slowly out until the bottom of the surface meniscus is level with the graduation mark. You now have exactly 5ml juice in the pipette and this is allowed to run into the conical flask which has previously been rinsed with distilled water. Be careful not to splash the sides and when the pipette has finished dripping, lightly touch the surface of the juice with the tip of the pipette to draw out the last drop (do not blow it out). Next add approximately 25ml distilled water and two drops only of 1% phenolphthalein solution (if you are dealing with a coloured juice either previously de-colourise a quantity by shaking it with a teaspoon of activated charcoal or use litmus paper in place of phenolphthalein).

The graduated burette is then filled with decinormal sodium hydroxide solution. Take care with this liquid, it is caustic. If you have filled

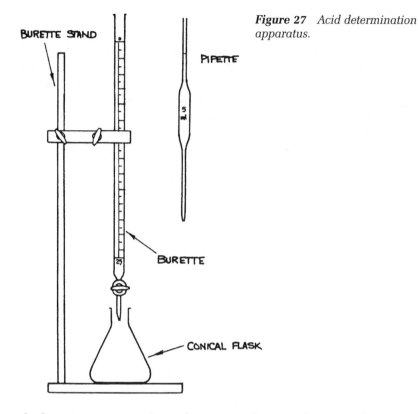

**Figure 27** *Acid determination apparatus.*

BURETTE STAND

PIPETTE

BURETTE

CONICAL FLASK

the burette to a point above the zero mark, open the tap and run some of the contents out into a container until the level is at or below the zero mark. Next note the level in the burette and place the conical flask beneath the tap. The sodium hydroxide solution is run, a little at a time, into the flask which is frequently, but gently, shaken to mix the contents. As soon as the contents take on a pink colour which fails to disappear on shaking, or if you are using litmus, when it changes from red to blue, you have reached the neutral point and the level in the burette should be noted again. By subtracting the first reading from the second you can deduce the volume of sodium hydroxide that was required to neutralise the juice acid. Repeat the measurement two or three times to make sure that you are getting consistent results, then divide the average result by 10. The figure you arrive at is the acidity of the juice expressed as % sulphuric acid. If this figure is below 0.65% the acidity of your juice needs no reduction but if it is higher steps must be taken to bring it down.

The acids in your juice will be mainly tartaric and malic acids. Acid reduction by means of chalk is perfectly satisfactory as long as it is not overdosed. The first acid to be neutralised by chalk will be the tartaric acid and you may remove all this acid without ill effect, but if any of the malic acid is reduced in this way calcium salts are formed which affect the taste adversely. When grapes are fully ripe most of the acid in the juice will be tartaric, but the less ripe the grapes the higher will be the proportion of malic acid. It is probably safe to assume that at least 25% of the acidity will be tartaric, and as all of this can safely be removed with chalk, if the acidity is less than 0.88% an addition of precipitated chalk will solve the problem – 4.6g of chalk will reduce the acidity of one gallon by 0.1%.

If the juice acidity is higher than 0.88%, the safest way for the amateur to reduce further acidity is by dilution with water. This should seldom be necessary and if your grapes are consistently over-acid, you should grow an earlier variety.

When sugar and acid adjustments have been made the juice is allowed to stand undisturbed for up to 48 hours. During this period the suspended solids will settle out leaving almost clear juice above a fluffy deposit of pulp. It is only necessary now to carefully siphon or pump the clear must into a clean fermenting vessel leaving behind as much of the 'fluff' as possible.

## Must destined for red or rosé wine

We have already seen that with the exception of a few hybrids, black grapes have white juice. If a red or rosé wine is to be made the colour must be extracted from the skins.

Red and rosé musts therefore differ from white in that the initial fermentation is carried out on the whole pulp and not just the juice. The red pigment in the skin is readily soluble in alcohol and the ethanol produced in the early ferment is able to extract it. The deeper the colour required, the longer needs to be the period on the skins. However depth of colour should not be the criterion. Apart from colouring matter, tannin and other compounds are also extracted and a really deep red colouration in wine from grapes grown in our climate will often be associated with harshness and unpalatability. If in doubt it is always better to err on the pale side. Three days on the pulp is recommended as the maximum in this country.

Black grapes must first be stripped from the stalks as these are high in tannin and should not be allowed to remain in contact with the fermenting pulp. When the time is right to press these grapes their slipperiness will have disappeared and the stabilising action of the stalks will not be required. The separated grapes are milled into a wooden vat or polythene bin where they are sulphited at the same rate as white juice – 1g sodium metabisulphite per gallon of pulp.

A portion of juice is drained off so that the acid and sugar content may be measured and corrected in the same way as described for white musts. Should you be dealing with a coloured juice it will be necessary to de-colourise a portion with activated charcoal before titrating for acidity. This is done by shaking a teaspoon of charcoal in about 50ml juice for a few moments, then allowing it to stand while the charcoal settles out.

After correction for acidity and sugar if necessary, the must is ready for yeast inoculation.

# ය 13 The fermentation

## Theory

Even today, with all the armoury of modern science, we do not yet fully understand every step in the process of alcoholic fermentation.

The metamorphosis from juice to wine is often thought of as a simple reaction in which the sugar in the juice is converted into roughly equal proportions by weight of alcohol and carbon dioxide. In general terms this is the result and it may be expressed chemically as follows:

$$C_6H_{12}O_6 \quad = \quad 2C_2H_5OH \quad + \quad 2CO_2$$

| glucose and fructose | ethyl alcohol | carbon dioxide |
|---|---|---|
| (100 parts by weight) | (51.1 parts by weight) | (48.9 parts by weight) |

In reality, the whole process passes through several complex stages and a host of other compounds are involved. I am not going to delve deeply into wine chemistry here because it will be of little interest to many readers, and in any case it would need a much larger book to deal with it. Nevertheless a brief outline of the fermentation and its products will help the novice to appreciate the miracle which takes place in the winery.

Yeasts contain several compounds known as enzymes, which may be fairly described as biological catalysts. Each is capable of stimulating a specific chemical reaction and the fermentation of grape juice

**A simplified scheme of the fermentation process**

| Stage | Compond | Enzyme | Product |
|---|---|---|---|
| 1 | Glucose and fructose (6 carbon atoms per molecule) | Hexokinase and adolase | Triose sugars (3 carbon atoms per molecule) |
| 2 | Triose sugars | Oxidoreductase | Glycerine and glyceric acid |
| 3 | Glyceric acid | Enolase | Pyruvic acid |
| 4 | Pyruvic acid | Carboxylase | Acetaldehyde and carbon dioxide |
| 5 | Acetaldehyde | Zymas | Alcohol Glyceric acid (back to stage 3) Succinic acid and alcohol |

involves six or more of these enzymes. In a very *simplified* form the process may be summarised as shown in the table.

There are five main steps in the transition from sugar to alcohol and carbon dioxide. Watching a bubbling ferment this may be hard to believe, but of course all five steps are happening simultaneously with countless millions of different sugar molecules. It has been calculated that one yeast cell, 5,000 of which could be laid end to end in an inch, provides the enzymes for the breakdown of 10,000 sugar molecules every second. We owe much indeed to this humble life-form.

Some of the original constituents of grape juice, such as citric acid, disappear during fermentation while others like succinic acid make their appearance. The table on the opposite page gives a breakdown of the main constituents of a finished wine. The balance of these constituents will vary according to several factors such as the original grape variety, its maturity at harvest and the speed of the ferment.

## Practice

It is often said that theory and practice are different animals. Certainly if the vintner proceeds with care, the practice of winemaking will not seem so daunting as the theory might suggest. After all vinting has gone on for 5,000 years or so and for 4,900 of those years *nothing* was known

**The main constituents of finished wine**

| Constituent | Content | Property |
|---|---|---|
| Water | 75–92% | Acts as a solvent and prevents immediate death from imbibing neat alcohol! |
| Ethyl alcohol | 8–20% | Acts as a solvent and preservative. Toxic but pleasant in limited quantities |
| Carbon dioxide | 0.05–0.15% | Adds life and freshness to wine |
| Glycerine | 1–2% | Adds mellowness and roundness. Only very noticeable in wines made from *botrytis*-infected grapes |
| Acetaldehyde | 25–45 mg/l | Noticeable in sherry, but not beneficial in excess in light table wines. Often indicates acetic spoilage |
| Other aldehydes | traces | Contribute to flavour and bouquet |
| Esters (e.g. Ethyl acetate) | 50–150mg/l | Contribute to flavour and bouquet |
| Higher alcohols | up to 0.2% | Contribute to flavour, bouquet and hangovers! |
| Acetic acid | 0.03–0.08% | Present in all wines. Beneficial in tiny quantities but ruins wine in excess |
| Tartaric acid Malic acid Succinic acid Lactic acid | 0.3–0.6% combined | Gives wine zest and life. Aids preservation |
| Unfermentable sugars | | 0.1% Little effect |
| Unfermented sugars | | Very variable. Affects sweetness or dryness of wine |

of yeasts or enzymes. Our newly acquired knowledge has, if anything, simplified our task and we are now able to make wines far superior to any that the ancients knew.

## The white ferment

In the winery our fermenting vessel of prepared juice is now ready for inoculation with the active yeast starter. The ideal temperature for starting a ferment is in the region of 18°C–21°C, but as we have seen already high quality yeasts are able to work in very cool conditions. We frequently started ferments at around 12°C. If you are working in a winery which is very cold you may raise the temperature of the must by the following method.

Siphon out a quantity of juice into a large stainless steel or aluminium container. Heat this to 50°C–60°C on a cooker, being careful to stir constantly to avoid overheating, then stir the heated portion back into the bulk. Do not stew the warmed portion and do not raise the temperature of the main bulk to more than about 20°C. An over-active ferment must be avoided and once warm a large active bulk will not cool naturally as the ferment itself creates heat.

Do not expect the juice to explode into immediate activity as soon as you add the yeast. There may still be a fairly high level of sulphur dioxide there which, although it will not kill the yeast, may retard it for a while. Gradually the sulphur dioxide will become exhausted and when it falls below a certain level the ferment will start. Do not worry about the waiting period; after all, if the yeast will not work nothing else will, since bacteria and wild yeasts are far more vulnerable to sulphur dioxide. If the ferment has not started after a week it probably means that you overdosed the metabisulphite earlier and an aerating racking should remedy the situation.

Once the ferment starts the temperature of the space in which the fermentation vessel is placed should be reduced to around 13°C–16°C. The outside winery in late October and November will seldom need cooling in our climate! Nevertheless, a vessel in a sheltered position, lying in the path of full sunlight pouring through an open door or window could easily overheat, and such conditions should not be allowed to occur. If the fermentation takes place at too high a temperature it will be very violent and it will work itself out too quickly. If this is not avoided much of the bouquet and character of the wine will be lost. Indeed if the ferment overheats greatly, it may even reach a temperature where the yeast is killed. Remember that grape juice is the perfect medium for yeast and you will not need to add nutrients. The main task is to control the speed of the ferment rather than boost it. The ideal fermentation period is generally about three weeks and unless the temperature is very low it will seldom take longer.

## Racking

When the fermentation has quite ceased the wine is allowed to stand for up to six weeks and then it should be carefully racked off the dead yeast into a clean vessel. *Never* allow the wine to rest on the old yeast for longer than six weeks or you will run the risk of a yeast casse, easily recognised by a disgusting 'mousey' flavour and aftertaste in the wine. This is caused by the enzymes in the yeast digesting the yeast cells themselves and the results are disastrous.

Carry out racking with as little splashing and disturbance as possible. The wine may still be a little hazy due to suspended matter but you do not want to make it worse by accidentally rousing the old yeast lees. Make sure that the new vessel is topped up well to prevent too much contact with air and fit a clean bung and lock. Although the ferment is finished you will find it useful to use a lock until the stabilisation of the wine is complete. Stabilisation should commence immediately as described in the next chapter.

## Red and rosé ferments

This differs markedly from the white ferment only in the initial stages. The milled pulp is sulphited and checked for sugar and acid as detailed in Chapter 12. As the sulphur dioxide content of the pulp will be fairly high to start with, it is a good idea to leave the covered pulp bin or vat to stand for twenty-four hours before inoculating the yeast starter. This waiting period will also give the enzymes present in the grape pulp time to break down the pulp and skin walls rendering colour and juice extraction easier.

The period of fermentation on the pulp may be as little as one day and should seldom be left for more than three, for the reasons explained earlier. The ferment will quickly form a pulp cap on the surface and this should be turned twice a day to aid even colour extraction and reduce the likelihood of acetification. As soon as it is considered that sufficient colour has been extracted by the juice the fermenting pulp is pressed. The frothing juice is run off into a clean fermenting vessel and henceforth treated in the same way as white juice as described earlier in this chapter.

# ∽ 14 Stabilisation and preparation for the bottle

## Chemical stability

Just as it was vital to preserve the qualities of the juice from spoilage, so too must your wine be preserved. There are several potential hazards which must be prevented by means of careful stabilisation before bottling.

### *Free sulphur dioxide content*

Most of the protective sulphur dioxide added to the original must will have disappeared by now and it is essential that it is replaced without more ado. Unlike juice which is shortly to be fermented, wine needs to be protected until it is drunk and this may be for a period of several years. It is therefore necessary to be certain that the level of active sulphur dioxide in the wine is correct – too little and the wine will not keep, too much and the taste will be affected.

Fortunately the measurement and adjustment of active sulphur dioxide is very simple. Suppliers of the necessary apparatus and chemicals for this test and all others mentioned in this chapter are given in Appendix A. In fact, sulphur dioxide in wine is in two forms: 'bound' and 'free'. When first added to wine, some of it ends up bound to aldehydes and sugars, and in this form it is inactive. However, once these compounds are saturated further additions of sulphur dioxide end

**Figure 28**   *Free sulphur dioxide determination cylinder.*

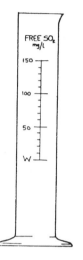

up in the form of sulphurous acid. This is able to combine with oxygen thus preventing the oxidation of other compounds in the wine and at the same time removing the oxygen necessary to sustain aerobic spoilage organisms. It also possesses antiseptic properties which, although slight, work beneficially in conjunction with its reducing properties. The sulphur dioxide, which is in the form of sulphurous acid, is called *free* sulphur dioxide. Its measurement is described here.

## Test for sulphur dioxide

*Apparatus*
Sulphur dioxide measuring cylinder
Pipette

*Reagents*
Blue solution (a stabilised iodine solution with a shelf-life of approximately two months)

*Method*
Wine is poured into the cylinder up to the graduated mark 'W' (or, in some patterns, the zero mark). Blue solution is then added a few drops

at a time from the pipette. After each addition a thumb is held over the mouth of the cylinder and the contents are shaken, care being taken to avoid spillage.

As soon as the blue colour persists for more than a few seconds after shaking, the new level in the cylinder is noted from the calibrated scale. This will give you a direct reading denoting the free sulphur dioxide content of the wine in milligrams per litre.

There *are* more accurate methods of determination, but if this method is carried out carefully and repeated to check your results, it is perfectly adequate for most purposes.

White wines should contain about 50 mg/l and red and rosé wines about 40 mg/l. If the content is raised to more than 70 mg/l it will be detectable on the palate and this must be avoided.

## *Adjustment of the free sulphur dioxide level*

Sulphur dioxide will be released into the wine by the addition of sodium or potassium metabisulphite. The sodium salt, which is preferable for reasons I shall mention later, contains about 60% sulphur dioxide by weight. Therefore by knowing the volume of your wine and its sulphur dioxide content, you may easily calculate the necessary addition of sodium metabisulphite to raise the free sulphur dioxide content to the desired level.

Anyone who can read a hydrometer and make the required sugar addition for chaptalisation will be able to measure the free sulphur dioxide content of their wine and make corrections if necessary. A typical example is given here to illustrate the procedure.

*Example*
Five gallons of white wine have a measured free sulphur dioxide content of 10 mg/l.

Requirement: to raise the level to 50 mg/l.

Calculation:
- Volume of wine    = 5 gallons
                           = 5 × 4.546 litres
                           = 22.73 litres

- Free $SO_2$ content required
  Free $SO_2$ content measured
  Therefore $SO_2$ addition required

  = 50 mg/l
  =10 mg/l
  = 40 mg/l

- Therefore total $SO_2$ addition required = 40 × 22.73 mg
  = 40 × 22.73 ÷ 1000g
  = 0.9092g

- Sodium metabisulphite contains approximately 60% $SO_2$. Therefore, the addition of sodium metabisulphite required to yield 0.9092g $SO_2$ is:

$$\frac{100}{60} \times 0.9092 = 1.515 \text{ g}$$

In fact an addition of 1.5g will be accurate enough.

This addition is dissolved in a small quantity of wine and then stirred into the bulk. After resting for twenty-four hours another free sulphur dioxide measurement should be taken to ensure that the right correction has been made. Once you have satisfied yourself on this point you may rest assured that the wine is at least safe from oxidation and bacterial spoilage but it is still necessary to take certain other measures.

Although not always the case, the wine may by this time have fallen clear and bright and novices could be forgiven for bottling straight away. However, there is a strong possibility that they would be unpleasantly surprised later if they did. It is very rare that a wine after fermentation is so perfectly balanced that it requires no stabilisation before bottling. After all, it is a complex mixture of many compounds in solution – some affect each other and some are unstable and liable to appear in troublesome forms if present in excess, or under certain conditions of temperature. For this reason you must, as far as possible, correct imbalances which are later likely to throw hazes or deposits.

## Tartrate stabilisation

As soon as the free sulphur dioxide content has been checked and adjusted the temperature of the wine should be lowered for a period of several weeks. Artificial refrigeration can shorten this period but I am assuming that most amateurs will have to rely on the climate to cool their wine. As the season will now be approaching the coldest period of the year there should be no problems. Very small quantities can be lifted bodily into a cold place and large volumes in the outside winery may be cooled by merely leaving the door open at night.

Due to the wine's alcohol content its freezing point will be depressed to around –4°C and its temperature should therefore not be allowed to fall below this or it will freeze and may rupture the container. If a particularly cold spell occurs do not leave a small carboy in the open or you may end up with a giant wine-lolly wrapped in shattered glass! In such conditions a closed outside winery will usually offer adequate frost protection, especially to large bulks which will not freeze easily anyway.

The main aim of this cooling is to precipitate as much unstable tartrate as possible in order to avoid the chance of it crystalising later in the bottle. If your wine is in a glass vessel you will soon notice the appearance of small crystals on the bottom and sometimes the sides. These crystals are the potassium and calcium salts of tartaric acid which are insoluble at low temperatures. The colder your wine the more tartrates will be thrown out. The crystals are colourless though they will readily become tinted with colouring matter in the wine.

It is worth mentioning here that *sodium* tartrate salts are soluble at much lower temperatures, and it is for this reason that sodium metabisulphite should be used in preference to potassium metabisulphite when adjusting sulphur dioxide levels. The addition of potassium ions increases the likelihood of tartrate instability.

Before the weather warms up again. the tartrate-stabilised wine must be racked off the precipitated crystals or they will slowly go back into solution.

If for some reason it is impracticable to cool your wine much, for example a hogshead in a house cellar, it is a sensible precaution to carry out a simple test to see whether your wine has an excessively unstable tartrate content. A wine sample is placed in a small bottle or test tube which should be kept in the bottom compartment of your refrigerator for a week. The appearance of crystals indicates instability and, as you are unable to remove this by cooling, it must be held in check chemically. The addition of approximately 0.5g metatartaric acid per gallon of wine will prevent tartrate precipitation for up to eighteen months.

If, in spite of all precautions, crystals do appear in the bottle do not worry unduly for the taste will be unimpaired. Just ensure that you decant the wine from the crystals when you pour it. Although tasteless they are a trifle gritty.

## Fining

Fortunately times have changed, but I remember in my early days as a country winemaker being told by more experienced people who should have known better that "fining is unnecessary if you have made your wine properly". Humbug! If you make a wine from nature's products they will vary every year. The natural balance of their constituents will depend on the season they were grown in and fining is often essential unless you are satisfied with an inferior product.

If fining is carried out badly it is true that the wine will suffer, just as a badly chaptalised or sulphited wine will. *Any* addition made to juice or wine must be done on a calculated basis or you can do more harm than good, but fining has been carried out in better wines for centuries and its omission will frequently lead to a disappointing product.

Certain compounds may suddenly appear in a wine in the form of hazes. They do not settle out naturally and cannot be filtered out. They consist of millions of tiny particles, each of which carries an electro-static charge of the same polarity as its neighbours. These hazes are called 'colloids' and some are negatively charged while others are posi-tively charged. In either case flocculation and precipitation is prevented due to the fact that like charges repel each other. Filtering is useless as the particles are far too small to be trapped. The only answer is fining by the calculated addition of a substance carrying the opposite electro-static charge. Results are rapid – the opposing charges attract each other and flocculation and precipitation occurs leaving a bright stable wine behind. Often we fine an apparently bright wine because tests have shown that invisible but unstable compounds exist in solution, which if left alone may quickly appear with a small temperature change.

It is important that any fining substance added to the wine should be used in calculated quantities. Under-fining will fail to totally remove the instability and over-fining will introduce new problems or perhaps "tear the coat from the wine" as the Germans say. Failure to fine at all may result in unsightly hazes or deposits appearing in what you originally bottled as a star-bright product. Although the taste may be unaffected, it is embarrassing to say the least to pour a friend a glass of high quality soup.

## Protein stability test

One of the commonest causes of hazes is an excessive protein content – this is particularly true of northern wines – and a simple test will establish whether your wine needs treatment.
Filter a small sample of wine into a clear glass bottle or test tube and incubate it at 70°C for 15 minutes. This can easily be done with the aid of a saucepan of water and a thermometer. The water is heated to 70°C and the sample container is immersed in it for the desired period. Do not forget to allow time for the wine sample to attain the same temperature as that of the bath. After which the sample is cooled and examined for the appearance of any cloudiness. If present, protein instability exists.
Protein colloids are positively charged so it is necessary to make an addition of negatively charged particles to remove them. The best treatment in this case is a measured dose of suspended bentonite. The addition required will normally be between two and five grams per gallon of wine. The correct amount is established by a simple test.

*Apparatus required*
4 small clear glass bottles or beakers
4 test tubes
Graduated 5ml pipette 50 ml pipette.

First make up a 1% bentonite suspension by shaking 1g bentonite in 100ml water. Bentonite is awkward stuff to wet and it is best dispersed by standing for one or two hours with occasional shaking until an even suspension is achieved.
Pipette four 50ml wine samples into separate glass bottles or beakers. With the aid of the graduated 5ml pipette add 2, 3, 4 and 5ml shaken 1% bentonite suspension into respective samples and mark each accordingly. Stir the samples to ensure an even dispersion of bentonite then allow them to stand for two days. Next pipette off a little of the cleared portion of each sample into four separate test tubes, again marking the tubes to indicate which is which. The test tubes are then

incubated as before at 70°C for fifteen minutes. After cooling, the samples are examined – that which has had the lowest bentonite addition and remains unclouded has been correctly dosed. The number of millilitres of bentonite added to that particular sample is equal to the number of grams of bentonite that must be added to each gallon of wine.

## Protein fining treatment

The previously determined quantity of bentonite is mixed into about ten times its own weight of wine. This process is eased considerably by the use of a hand-held egg whisk or electric mixer used every twenty minutes or so while the mixture stands for an hour or two. The standing time is necessary to allow the bentonite time to swell and wet. When an even dispersion has been obtained the main bulk of the wine is thoroughly roused and the bentonite dose is stirred in. The wine is allowed to stand for about a fortnight after which the clear protein-stabilised wine is carefully racked off. Care is needed because the bentonite sediment is rather fluffy and easily disturbed.

## Gelatine/tannin fining

Bentonite being negatively charged is capable of treating positively charged colloids such as protein hazes, but not all colloids are positively charged. Colouring matter and tannin complexes, for example, are negatively charged and these too can cause hazes or harshness if present in excess.

In this case we must resort to a positively charged fining agent and one of the most popular and effective is gelatine. If gelatine is used on its own however it will remove much of the necessary wine tannin and leave the wine flaccid on the palate. Sometimes it is necessary to reduce the tannin in the wine but it must not be stripped out completely. For this reason tannin, in the form of tannic acid, is added to the wine at the same time as gelatine.

If it is your opinion that the wine tannin is naturally well balanced, gelatine and tannin should be added in equal quantities. If, on the other hand, you feel that the wine has excessive tannin then tannic acid is added at a lower rate than that of the gelatine. Your palate will tell you if the tannin content is too high as it is indicated by a distinctive hard flavour which cannot be confused with acidity. Should you wish to reduce the wine tannin content, reduce the tannic acid quantity to between 50% and 75% of the gelatine addition. Tests on small quantities followed by tasting is the simplest way of establishing the most suitable ratio.

## Gelatine fining test

The first thing to do is to establish whether gelatine fining is needed at all. Excessive tannin will require it as will a wine which remains hazy after bentonite fining. Make up 1% tannic acid BP and 1% gelatine BP solutions. Tannic acid will readily dissolve in cold water, but gelatine dissolves more easily in hot, but not boiling water.

Equal quantities of these solutions are added to four separate wine samples in exactly the same way as described for bentonite, the only difference being that incubation is not required. Once the lowest addition of gelatine necessary to precipitate the haze is established the gelatine/tannin ratio is determined as detailed above.

Sometimes gelatine/tannin treatment is unnecessary either to remove a haze or to reduce the natural wine tannin content. It can nevertheless still be used to advantage as a means of speeding a bentonite fining precipitation. If all three agents are used the gelatine/tannic acid fining is stirred into the wine six hours *after* the bentonite. By this method clarification of the wine should be complete in 2–3 days instead of the 7–10 days usual for bentonite alone.

## Heavy metals

If your vinification has been carried out carefully and every attempt has been made to avoid metal contamination, your wine should be free from excessive metal concentrations. However, it needs only *very* small concentrations of some metals to cause troubles. Copper and iron particularly are responsible for the formation of metal casses which are brown and grey deposits respectively. The commercial limit for iron in wine is only eight parts per million and for copper two parts per million.

Fining excess heavy metals from a wine is not really for the amateur as it entails 'blue fining' with potassium ferrocyanide. Over-use results in the formation of prussic acid and there are limits to the amount of kick your wine should have! If your wine suffers badly from heavy metal contamination send a sample to professional analysts for a recommended dose of ferrocyanide and a further sample after treatment to ensure your wine has not been overdosed.

The best defence against heavy metal contamination is vigilant vinting. Ensure that iron and mild steel parts of mills and presses for example are painted. Iron may also be picked up from sources such as rusty barrel hoops. Copper is generally less of a hazard as copper-containing materials are less likely to come into contact with juice and wine. Articles such as bronze pump-housings are comparatively inert and contact is only momentary anyway.

## Maderisation

This is really a polite word for oxidation. It is most likely to be encountered in senile wines or young wines which have an inadequate sulphur dioxide content. It is easily recognised in white wines by a lack of freshness, the appearance of a sherry-like flavour and a darkening of the colour. In white wine from northern regions it is disastrous and the vintner commits a cardinal crime if he allows it to occur, for his wine's character will be utterly destroyed.

## Biological stability

Wine can be host to, and the victim of, a large army of invaders. These fall into two main groups: bacteria and yeasts.

## Bacteria

Fortunately most wine spoilage bacteria are aerobic i.e. they require oxygen to survive. This being so, an adequate level of free sulphur dioxide in the wine will give a high degree of protection. A few of the more commonly met bacterial hazards are discussed here.

## Acetic ferments

Acetobacter aceti produce acetic acid or vinegar. However superior wine vinegar may be to malt vinegar, we do not wish to produce it here! Prevention of attack is assured by maintaining a concentration of free sulphur dioxide in excess of 30 mg/l. It is vital that an acetic ferment should be avoided as it is irreversible and it is impossible to remove the acetic acid from the wine once it is formed.

All wines contain traces of acetic acid as a byproduct of a well regulated alcoholic ferment, but an excess will ruin the wine. A white wine with more than 0.12% acetic acid is normally unpalatable. Red and rosé wines are particularly vulnerable to attack early in the vinification when fermenting on the pulp due to the necessarily low sulphur dioxide level at that time, and the inevitable contact with the air. This is another good reason for limiting the period of pulp fermentation.

## Mannitic ferments

These are due to mannitic bacteria which thrive in conditions of warmth and low acidity and in the presence of unfermented sugar. The products are lactic and acetic acids, glycerol, carbon dioxide and mannitol which has a particularly unpleasant smell and taste. Prevention is aided by achieving an adequate wine acidity and by storing the wine in a cool place.

## Propionic ferments

An infection leading to a condition known as 'tourne', but unlikely to occur in wines with an adequate acid and tannin content. The symptoms are the appearance of a silky sheen in the wine when agitated and loss of life, flavour and bouquet, due partly to the breakdown of tartaric acid.

## Graisse

A condition caused by *Micrococcus viscosus vini* which results in a rather repulsive slimy stringiness in the wine. It is again prevented by an adequate sulphur dioxide content.

## Malolactic ferments

Caused by lactic bacteria, (mainly *Bacterium gracile*), these ferments can have a beneficial effect by reducing excess acidity by converting the wine's malic acid into lactic acid which is softer on the palate. At the same time carbon dioxide is produced. The slightly sparkling or 'spritzig' character of some Mosel wines is partly due to this cause.

An attempt to induce malolactic fermentation is not always successful and there is always the danger that a malignant infection will replace or accompany that required. This is due to the fact that lactic bacteria are very susceptible to sulphur dioxide and if the level of this protective agent is kept low to give the lactic bacteria a chance, other bacteria may invade the wine. Certainly it is safer for the amateur to keep the sulphur dioxide level up rather than attempt a malolactic ferment.

## Yeasts

All wild yeasts are dealt with adequately by sulphur dioxide, but good strains of wine yeast will survive in very high concentrations of this compound and their control, when necessary, is discussed here.

## Sweetening wine and the stability of wine in the presence of sugar

Normally a wine will ferment out dry or have very little residual sugar. Many people like wines in this natural state but others prefer their wines sweeter. Before the Second World War German Hocks and Mosel wines were almost always sold naturally dry. After the war, perhaps due to the rarity of sweet foods in that period, the public demanded wines that had a little sugar in them. Currently there is a reversal in this trend and more and more people, especially regular wine drinkers, are asking for drier wines again.

Wines do not change in character to suit the public demand purely by magic – they are altered to meet the market. There is therefore nothing to stop you sweetening your wine to suit your own palate, just as most German table wines are currently sweetened to meet popular demand. Commercial wines may only be sweetened by using some of the original grape sugar, but as an amateur you can use the much simpler process of stirring in white granulated sugar. Unless you sugar your wines very heavily, the difference between the taste of sucrose and fruit sugar is unnoticeable.

The amount of sugar you add depends on your own palate and your best course is to add a measured quantity, a little at a time, until the desired sweetness has been achieved. Be cautious. If you over-sweeten the main bulk of your wine you are stuck with it – short of restarting the ferment! If your wine is quite dry to start with, an addition of about 30g or 1oz sugar per gallon will be enough to take the edge off the dryness. Try this addition first and only add more if you think you need it.

A sweetened wine, or one containing natural residual sugar, needs special treatment before bottling. It is a fermentable liquid once more and its biological stability must be assured before the cork is pushed home. If it is not there is a strong possibility that fermentation will occur in the bottle. This will not only cause a little sediment due to yeast multiplication but will also remove the sugar you were at pains to introduce! As mentioned earlier it is useless relying on sulphur dioxide to do the job. The level of sulphur dioxide needed to kill wine yeasts is so high that it can be tasted. There are however two possibilities open to the amateur winemaker.

Firstly the sweetened wine may be 'sterile bottled'. This entails passing the wine through a filter capable of removing all yeast cells, into bottles that have been rinsed with strong metabisulphite solution (described later). Fortunately there are now several suitable filters on the market which will satisfactorily cope with small quantities of wine. The hogshead producer will find these small filters quite inadequate and it will be necessary to hire or purchase a filter and pump (see Appendix A).

Secondly the vintner may resort to 'thermotic bottling'. This is similar to the pasteurising process. In the commercial field there are special machines designed to do the job but the amateur can get by using a simplified process. The wine is bottled, but not corked, and its temperature is then raised to 50°C–55°C by immersing the bottles up to their necks in a waterbath or large saucepan for ten minutes or so. This will kill all yeasts remaining in the wine without cooking it. It is then cooled and corked – with sterilised corks of course!

Before thermotic bottling it is essential to make sure that the wine is protein stable at that temperature but this should have been done earlier anyway.

## *Blending wines*

If it is intended to blend the products of two vine varieties for example, it is best done at the juice stage. Sometimes, however, it may be decided to blend two finished wines which were originally destined for separate bottling. It is seldom wise to make a witches brew of more than two wines unless they come from the same grape – too many varieties in one wine can lead to a confusion of flavours which blurs any good characteristics.

Always blend sample quantities before you proceed with the bulk. The result may not come out quite as you might have expected. You may feel otherwise but I think it is unwise to try to raise the quality of a poor wine by blending it with a particularly good one. The result at best is two bottles of mediocre wine for every bottle of good wine you had before – a poor exchange.

Wines made from the same grape or from compatible varieties such as Mueller-Thurgau and Seyval Blanc can often be blended to their mutual advantage. It may be that in a certain year the Mueller-Thurgau crop is left on the vine too long and its acid value has fallen low enough to make a rather flat wine. It might well be that an addition of wine produced from the higher acidity, but more neutral-charactered, Seyval would yield a blend of balanced acidity and good character.

Blends should be rested for a little while before bottling and their stability should be checked and adjusted if necessary.

# ᘓ 15 Bottling, maturing and storage

Bottling should be carried out in surroundings which are as clean as possible. This will present few difficulties to the small producer but if you have to deal with a large bulk in an outside cellar it is a good plan to wash everything down first, at least with clean water to lay the dust, but preferably with a 1:100 solution of hypochlorite. On the other hand avoid strongly scented antiseptics or you may find the wine is tainted – a carbolic bouquet is hardly in character!

Just before bottling, the free sulphur dioxide level should be finally checked and adjusted if necessary as described at the beginning of Chapter 14.

## Bottles

Anyone who is keen enough to grow their own wine is unlikely to put their product into orange squash or gin bottles, but the presentation of the wine should be taken seriously. Most people prefer to drink milk from a glass rather than a cup and the same psychology applies to wine bottles. Unfortunately as English wine has only recently been reborn we have no traditional bottle in this country and with alarming talk of the coming of the 'Euro-bottle' it is unlikely we ever will have an English bottle. English wine more closely resembles German in character than any other and for this reason it 'looks right' in a German bottle. Whether you prefer the green Mosel or the brown Hock bottle is up to you. I am sure that some of you will think me pernickety, but pouring English white wine from a bottle designed to hold claret is liable to give the unsuspecting drinker the same effect as stepping on a stair that isn't there at the first mouthful. The container and its contents are quite out of character.

Incidentally, the Hock bottle is quite suitable for red or rosé wine as the red wine from the Middle Rhine is put in the same bottle as the white from that region. However, it is unusual to find German red in this country, and the use of Burgundy or claret bottles for English red wine will not seem out of place.

Those who have as much as a hogshead to bottle may have to buy new bottles – at least for the first vintage. This may be accomplished more easily by approaching a local bottler rather than a bottle manufacturer who will not normally deal with orders for less than 5,000 bottles. If new bottles are acquired it should not be assumed that they are either clean or sterile. The one or two gallon vintner will doubtless use second-hand bottles and these will certainly need washing. If there is any sign of dirt it should be removed by means of a bottle brush before sterilising. All bottles should be sterilised by rinsing or spraying the inside with a 2% sulphur dioxide solution. This is made up by dissolving approximately 32g sodium metabisulphite in a litre of water (or about 5oz/gallon) together with a pinch of citric acid. If you do not have the means of spraying fresh solution into each bottle the solution may be poured from one bottle to the next, swirling each to make sure they are rinsed thoroughly. Every ten bottles or so fresh solution from the bulk should be used or the sulphur dioxide will be quickly exhausted.

If you have two or three hundred bottles to deal with it is generally worth hiring a proper spray unit (see Appendix A). These simple mains-water pressure-operated units give a small effective spray of fresh solution as each bottle is pressed onto the nozzle and they save an enormous amount of time. There are also much cheaper lever-operated spray units available but it may be more sensible to buy rather than hire.

Once the bottles have been rinsed they should be stood inverted, with their necks clear of the ground, to drain for about fifteen minutes. This will allow the bulk of the sulphur dioxide gas to run out, avoiding the possibility of excessive gas pick-up by the wine. Clean upturned plastic beer crates make excellent draining racks.

## Corks

High quality two-inch corks should be used. They should be smooth, even grained and have as few pores as possible. Unless purchased in an already sterilised form they must be washed, soaked and sterilised before use. They should first be washed in several changes of hot water, but not too hot for your hand to bear. The heat will open the pores of the cork and aid dust removal. If the water is *too* hot the cork will lose some of its elasticity. When the rinsing water ceases to be markedly cloudy the corks should be soaked for two hours in a 1.5% sulphur dioxide solution. This solution is less strong than the bottle rinse because sulphur dioxide embrittles the corks and for this reason the two-hour soak should not be exceeded. The solution is made up by dissolving approximately 25g sodium metabisulphite in a litre of water (or about 3¾oz/gallon) with a pinch of citric acid.

It is important that the corks are fully submerged during the soak as their natural buoyancy will try to float them clear of the sterilising solution. A weighted lid or plate of some inert material will serve this purpose.

## The filter

The mini-filters now available to amateur winemakers carry their own instructions for use and these are quite suitable for dealing with a few gallons but large quantities will necessitate hiring a multiple unit and pump. Such filters come in two popular plate sizes – 20 × 20cm and 40 × 40cm. They may look a little daunting but are in fact quite simple – they are illustrated in Figs. 29 and 30.

When assembled, the filter sheets are clamped firmly between a series of grooved filter plates. Wine is pumped into one side of the unit and has to pass through the filter sheets before it can emerge from the outlet. If the wine were pumped direct to the filter the pump pressure would rupture the filter sheets. To reduce this pressure, a bypass circuit is fitted to the inlet side. By adjusting the valve on this bypass the pressure on the filter sheets can be reduced and the wine flow from the two-way filling tap at the outlet can be regulated to a comfortable working speed.

If there is a lot of suspended matter such as bentonite present, the

**Figure 29**  *Diagrammatic plan of filter circuit.*

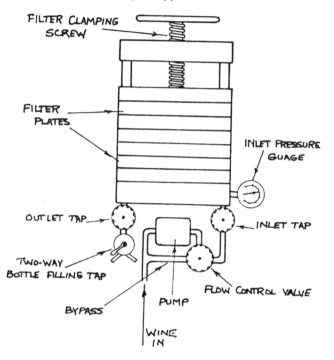

sheets may become clogged. The flow will then be restricted and the pressure on the sheets will build up with the risk of bursting them. This must not be allowed to occur and should the gauge indicate a pressure that cannot be adjusted to below 15lb/sq in. it is a sign that the sheets need replacing.

Whenever the pump is stopped the inlet valve should first be closed to prevent too rapid a pressure change on the sheets when the pump is switched on again. At such times the inlet valve is eased open after the pump is restarted.

## Filter sheets

If you wish to do no more than remove 'floaters' such as cask splinters and other miscellaneous flotsam, No. 5 filter sheets will be adequate.

**Figure 30** *Diagrammatic section through wine filter.*

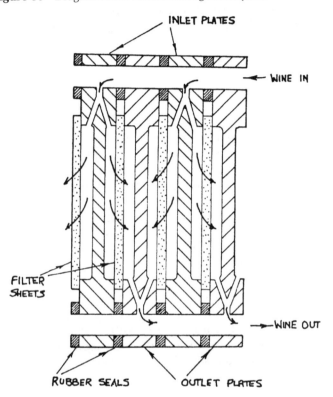

However, sterile bottling requires finer EK, or preferably M-EK sheets which will remove any organisms likely to cause a bottle ferment. The flow rate through these fine filter sheets should not exceed 15 gallons per sheet per hour (using 40cm filters).

## Sterilising the filter

If you intend to sterile bottle your wine, naturally the filter unit and sheets should be sterile themselves. The easiest procedure for the amateur is to pump a 2% sulphur dioxide solution though the assembled unit and then leave it to stand full for an hour before draining.

Unfortunately this method has a drawback in that the first one or two bottles to emerge will pick up excess sulphur dioxide and will have to be discarded. The only alternative procedure is to pass steam through the unit but this is not practicable for most amateurs as it requires a steam generator.

## Bottling

Before you commence any bottling operations it is essential to make sure you are properly organised. Of course, if you are only siphoning two gallons into a dozen bottles the degree of organisation needed is not very great, but even so you should ensure that everything you are likely to need is to hand.

When you have as much as a cask to cope with it is always a great help if there are two of you, especially if you are using a filter. One can then fill the bottles while the other corks them. The occasional break can be arranged for sterilising the next batch of bottles and for clearing the decks of those already corked.

In case things start to get out of hand it is wise to have a well-rehearsed emergency stop procedure. If you are unfamiliar with the equipment you do not want to waste time frantically turning off the wrong tap while your precious wine flows onto the floor. A dummy run using water is not as crazy as it sounds – you may then practise at no risk to your wine.

When filling your bottles it is important to leave as little air space between the wine and the cork as possible. Excessive air space will deplete the free sulphur dioxide rendering the wine vulnerable to spoilage.

## Corking

While the hand cork 'flogger' is suitable for a small number of bottles it is a very tedious method for large quantities. The 'Sanbri' or other types of small lever corkers are an improvement but anyone who is faced with two or three hundred bottles will probably find it worthwhile hiring a simple floor-standing corker. This can be adjusted to take any standard wine bottle and will considerably ease the work.

## Capsules

The most important function of a capsule is to protect the cork from attack by insects such as the cork moth, though undoubtedly capsules have an aesthetic appeal. Unquestionably lead capsules are the most functional and aesthetically pleasing, but they are seldom practical for the amateur as they require special and rather expensive machines to fit them. Nothing is more useless or more unsightly than a loosely fitted metal capsule.

Probably the most sensible capsules for amateur use are the 'Viscap' type. These shrink on to the bottle making a neat and effective seal. The only drawback with this type is that they are sensitive to moisture and if a cork weeps a little, the capsule will tend to become soft and tacky. Conversely they have a tendency to crack and split if they become too dry, nevertheless these hazards are seldom encountered if the wine is stored properly.

Do not become alarmed if you find a healthy mould growth on the cork when you remove the capsule prior to opening a bottle. Some wine will often seep through the cork and may support a vigorous mould colony under the capsule.

Unless the bottle has been stored upright allowing the cork to dry out, this will not invade the contents of the bottle. Even if it were able to do so the free sulphur dioxide in the wine would not allow it to survive.

## Labelling

Labels need not be applied immediately after bottling and if you insist on a spotless label at the table, labelling is best delayed to avoid the accumulation of cellar dirt. To my mind a little cellar grime in no way detracts from the appearance but if your storage space is on the damp side labels *can* become rather tatty after prolonged storage.

Unless you have a tame printer it is unlikely that you will have your own personal design, small quantities being so uneconomic. There is now a wide range of ready-printed labels available to the amateur and although some of them are hideous it should be possible to find a respectable design appropriate to your wine. If you are using German wine bottles, ensure that the height of your labels does not exceed 9cm or you will find they do not fit the contour of the bottle snugly.

## Storage

It is generally appreciated that wine is best stored at 10°C–13°C. More important however than actual temperature is temperature constancy. For example, storage at a constant temperature of 17°C is far better than a space where the temperature fluctuates rapidly between 0°C and 25°C. Roof-spaces are notorious for rapid and violent temperature changes and are usually quite unsuitable. Few will be fortunate enough to have a cellar these days but much can be done to avoid violent temperature changes by thermally insulating your wine storage space with one of the many materials now available.

## Binning

Bottles should always be laid on their side so that the wine is in contact with the cork. This will prevent the cork drying out, shrinking and allowing access of air and spoilage organisms.

**Figure 31** *Binning.*

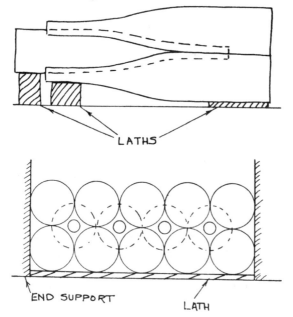

Small numbers of bottles may be laid in strong cardboard wine cartons as long as the storage area is dry. If it is damp the cases will soon collapse and breakage may result. Conventional wine racks are ideal but they tend to be costly if you are laying down any great number of bottles.

Undoubtedly the cheapest way of binning wine is to build a 'wall' of bottles as shown in Fig. 31. If you have never seen this method before it looks rather frightening but it is simple and quite safe. It is essential that the floor is level and that the ends of the bottle 'wall' are adequately supported of course, but it is possible to stack bottles up to five or six feet in this manner with very little chance of a breakage.

The first row of bottles is laid on laths on the floor between the end supports. The thickness of the laths must be such that the axis of the bottles is horizontal, the lath under the neck being thicker than the lath under the base. A further lath is laid in front of the necks of the first row so that a second row may rest with their base on this lath and the necks on the first row. These too should be horizontal. As long as the bottles are all of the same pattern they will nest together perfectly – naturally the system will not work with dissimilar bottles. A third row of bottles may now be laid on the first, and a fourth row on the second and so on. The use of further laths is generally unnecessary. If the 'wall' is built carefully it will be quite stable and there should be no excess load on any one bottle.

## Maturing

It is a widely held fallacy that the older a wine is the better it is. This idea holds good up to a point for very long-life wines such as the best clarets and vintage ports, but even they reach an age when their quality peak is passed. Northern table wines usually reach their peak early in life and are generally at their best with a bottle age of between one and five years.

Undoubtedly a little bottle age will improve your wine noticeably, allowing the development of its full flavour and bouquet. Resist the temptation to open your first bottle until the Christmas following the bottling. This means that a 1998 vintage should be drunk from Christmas 1999 onwards and that by the year 2003 the same wine will probably be on its way over the hill. Any wine must be given time to flower but it must not be allowed to run to seed.

# ෆ 16 Dessert, sparkling and pomace wine

Although primarily describing the vinification of still table wines much of the preceding chapters applies also to the production of dessert and sparkling wines. However, these specialities require some variations in skill and equipment and I would advise you to produce a good table wine before you attempt anything else. Nevertheless I will try to provide a few guidelines here for those who wish to try their hands at these wines. Pomace wine should not be despised and its production is described at the end of the chapter.

## Dessert wines

Perhaps it would be as well to begin by defining what we mean by dessert wines in this particular context. These products are typified by the German Auslese and quality French Sauternes. They are not fortified; they are almost always sweet and they possess their own characteristic flavour as a result of *botrytis* mildew infection of the crop.

The first essential for a dessert wine is a crop with a really high juice gravity. The second essential is the successful infection of that ripening crop by *botrytis*. If you attempt to make a dessert wine with a juice best destined for table wine merely by loading it with sugar, the result will be a sweet table wine – the distinctive flavour we seek will not be there.

The effect produced by *botrytis* is impossible to reproduce in any other way and it amounts to the difference between a £3.00 bottle of ordinaire Sauternes and maybe a £15–£20 bottle of Chateau Climens for example – it is hardly surprising that the mould is known as noble rot. The mould must not attack the crop before a certain degree of maturity is reached or the effect will be detrimental and *botrytis* mildew fungicides may be employed to keep it at bay until the juice gravity has reached around 65°0e. The mildew is then actually encouraged by means described in Chapter 3.

Apart from producing the special honey-like flavour, the mould will help to elevate the juice gravity by removing from the berries more water (and acid) than sugar. Naturally the juice quantity will be diminished as a result and it must be accepted that if you wish to make a dessert wine, you will have to be content with maybe only half the quantity you would produce if making a table wine. Nevertheless many will think the quality well worth the loss in quantity. An example of the effects of *botrytis* on the constitution of grape juice is given in the table below.

Only mould-infected bunches should be used for the must. Indeed certain types of these wines are made from selected berries! This helps contribute to their high cost. It is not possible to be too specific as to what final crop gravity is the lowest allowable for the production of a dessert wine but it is probably in the region of 100°0e. Even then it is most likely that the wine will ferment out naturally dry and sweetness will only be achieved by stopping the ferment prematurely or by sweetening the finished wine.

Ideally a dessert wine of the type we are aiming at should have an alcohol content of 12–14% by weight and a gravity of around 20°0e. This means that it is preferable to start with a juice gravity of around 120°0e. The garden grower using the right varieties stands a good chance of achieving this in a good year – due to the favourable microclimate a starting gravity will probably produce a naturally sweet wine although good yeasts may reduce even this level to dryness and the ferment may

**The effects of *Botrytis cinerea* on the constitution of grape juice**

| Property | Normally ripe grapes | *Botrytis* infected grapes |
|---|---|---|
| Volume of juice per kilo of grapes | 850ml | 500ml |
| Weight of sugar per litre of juice | 180g | 300g |
| Weight of acid (tartaric) per litre of juice | 5.5g | 5.0g |

have to be stopped artificially to retain the desired natural sugar. Although not allowed commercially, lesser gravities may be boosted by chaptalisation which may be preferred to sweetening afterwards. If chaptalisation is carried out it is wiser to make the necessary sugar addition after the ferment has started. This is due to the fact that the higher the gravity of a must is at the time of yeast inoculation, the slower will be the activation of the ferment. This is especially true when adding sugar that the yeast has to invert before it can use it. By chaptalising high gravity musts after the ferment has begun less of a workload is put on the yeast.

Once the ferment has started its progress must be watched so that the desired final gravity is not passed. This event is less likely and the wine will be improved if the speed of the ferment is slowed by cooling more than is usual with a table wine, although dessert wine ferments will usually be slower anyway.

Stopping the ferment at the desired moment may be accomplished by racking the wine off the yeast and passing it through a yeast-retaining filter. This is often less easy than it sounds as suspended yeast can quickly clog filters, and it is wise to use a coarse filter as a first stage. These wines are particularly prone to oxidation and the usual care must be taken to maintain the correct level of free sulphur dioxide.

## Sparkling wines

While dessert wines may be made using only simple table wine vinting equipment, sparkling wines need a few additional pieces of apparatus.

They contain much more carbon dioxide gas than the petillant table wines and commercially this is generated by one of three methods. The cheaper sparkling wines are often produced by impregnating still wines with gas. Except in quantities of a sodawater-bottleful at a time this method is impractical for the amateur. A second method whereby the bulk is fermented in a pressure vessel might be used by the more ingenious amateur, but undoubtedly the champenoise method is the most practicable. It is the oldest method of all and it is used for the finest champagnes. The process is summarised as follows.

## The must

Vine varieties likely to yield suitable sparkling wine musts have been discussed in Chapter 3 but an important property such musts should possess is a reasonable acidity. If the juice acidity is lower than 5–6g/l (expressed as sulphuric), it should be adjusted up to this level by a calculated addition of tartaric acid (1g/l tartaric acid is proportional to 0.653g/l sulphuric acid). A sparkling wine deficient in acid will lack zest.

## The fermentation

The first fermentation is carried out in the same way as described for table wines. The wine is then stabilised as described in Chapter 14 before being dosed for the secondary ferment.

It is probably wise to restrict the ultimate bottle pressure by ensuring that the sugar dosage never exceeds 18g sucrose, or granulated sugar, per litre of wine. Even so this will generate a pressure of about 3½ atmospheres in the bottle – or at least twice that normally found in bottled beer. The quantity of sugar necessary for your wine is calculated, dissolved in small amount of wine and then stirred into the bulk. A new yeast starter is then added.

The choice of a suitable yeast is particularly important here. First, it will have to start a ferment in a wine already containing around 11% alcohol. Secondly, it must form a sediment which is easily removed from the wine later and thirdly, it will spend a considerable period in the wine, and must produce no off flavours. Go to the trouble of buying a champagne yeast – several producers supply them.

The wine is usually bottled as soon as dosage and yeast inoculation has taken place but the amateur would be wise to await the start of the ferment in bulk before bottling. This will ensure that every bottle behaves in the same way and none will 'stick'. Do not delay bottling as soon as it is obvious the second ferment is active or some of the gas we wish to retain will be lost.

Due to the great pressure of generated carbon dioxide *only* thick champagne-type bottles should be used. I cannot stress this enough. In the days before the strong moulded champagne bottle, death and injury were frequent due to bottle explosions. Table wine bottles as sparkling wine containers are lethal. As you will doubtless be using secondhand bottles you should check them for chips and scratches, discarding any that are badly marked. If good bottles are used and dosage is not overdone there should be no danger of accidents, but the odd occasion can always arise and the use of heavy gloves and aprons and a face mask is a sensible precaution.

Unlike bottling a finished table wine where as little air space as possible is left, a gap of about 6cm should be left between the wine and the stopper. Hollow polythene stoppers should be used and they must be securely held in place by means of wire 'muselet' ties (see Appendix A). The wine is now laid down in a temperature of between 16°C and 20°C for a few days to encourage the fermentation. After a week it is either shifted to a cooler place or the temperature of the storage place is lowered – ideally to about 12°C.

The bottles should now lie on their sides for a period of a year. Once a month they should be gently shaken to dislodge the yeast sediment – do not be too vigorous with this shaking or you may encourage a burst. This will prevent the yeast becoming packed hard and render its removal easier later. At this stage the yeast will impart a little flavour to the wine and only champagne strains will produce the sought effect.

## Remuage

After a year's maturing you will have bottles of dry, sparkling wine containing a little yeast sediment. The next stage is remuage, or yeast concentration prior to removal.

After a final rousing the bottles are laid in racks so that they lie at an angle of approximately 45° with their punts uppermost. In the Champagne they use special racks or pupitres, but stout cardboard wine cases or some form of wine rack propped up at the correct angle will serve your purpose.

At two or three day intervals each bottle should be rotated slightly by twisting it a little one way then back a little more the other way. The action should result in turning the bottle about 45° from its last resting position. The object is to dislodge the yeast sediment and with each operation gradually work it down to the neck. The action should not be too violent or the yeast will tend to float up into the wine again. The granular nature of champagne yeasts will help prevent this and aid its progress towards the stopper, where it should end up in the hollow stem. Careful visual inspection from time to time will indicate how the settling is proceeding.

## *Disgorging*

Skilled cellarmen can disgorge the yeast from a bottle without resorting to freezing techniques but the amateur is strongly advised to use the neck-freezing method, or much of your labour is likely to end up on the floor.

In order to remove the yeast sediment cleanly from the wine we neatly encapsulate it in ice. This is done by immersing the necks of the bottles in a freezing mixture for a while.

Firstly the inverted bottles are cooled to about 6°C. Though it will mean working in batches if you are dealing with a large number of bottles, an hour in a kitchen refrigerator will be sufficient to achieve this. Cooling is necessary to reduce the pressure in the wine to a manageable level when the stopper is removed. The chilled bottles are next transferred, still inverted, to a rack resting on, or suspended over, a tray of freezing mixture so that approximately two inches of the necks are immersed in this mixture. Suitable wooden racks may be constructed without too much difficulty.

There are several possible freezing mixtures but without doubt the simplest is a mixture of one part cooking salt to three parts crushed ice. Enough ice can be made in the freezer compartment of a refrigerator to produce enough mixture for one or two dozen bottles. The efficiency of your freezing mixture will depend on the proportion of salt and ice and the size of the ice particles. The finer they are the better and it is worth a bit of effort crushing the ice well. The temperature of your mixture should settle down around −20°C. Between ten and twenty minutes' immersion in such a mixture should be sufficient to freeze the contents of the hollow stopper and a little more.

The yeast is now safely encapsulated and the bottles may be stood upright at last. Wash the salt from the necks to prevent it contaminating the wine and have your topping-up wine or syrup (described below) ready. Point the bottle away from you at an angle of 60° or so and ease off the muselet. If possible restrain the stopper from flying out with too much force to reduce the effervescence. Top up any air space with wine or syrup and quickly re-stopper to avoid excessive carbon dioxide loss. This time use a sterilised polythene stopper *without* a cavity. Wire on a new muselet and rinse the bottle in clean water. The bottles should now be laid down to recover from their assault.

## *Sweetening*

If topping-up wine is used instead of syrup the result will be a very dry (brut) wine which may not be to your taste. The palate is such an individual thing that one cannot be too specific on sweetening rates but everything mentioned in the discussion on sweetening table wines in Chapter 14 applies here. One variation however – the addition of syrup (sugar dissolved in wine) is more practical than the addition of sugar itself. This addition renders the wine fermentable again and as filtering is impossible, precautions should be taken to prevent further fermentation occurring by minimum delay and maximum hygiene.

## Pomace wine

After pressing your grapes to extract the juice for table or sparkling wine do not throw the pomace away. It is possible to make a delightful country wine with this material. If you do not have a reasonable quantity of pomace from your own crop, you may be able to purchase a quantity at small cost from a local vineyard. You will not normally obtain it free as it is usually spread back on the land as a high grade fertilizer.

The procedure for pomace wine is simple but great care must be taken to prevent oxidation which will ruin the freshness of this light wine. First, it is vitally important that the pomace is fresh from the press and has not been lying around for more than a few minutes. It should immediately be placed in a covered bin and sulphited at a rate of about 20g sodium metabisulphite per dustbinful.

Let us say that the pomace you have originally yielded 90 litres (20 gallons) of juice. You should add half that quantity, 45 litres (10 gallons), of water to the pomace and allow it to soak for two days well covered. Stirring should be minimised to prevent oxidation – prodding is a safer way of agitating it. After two days the pomace is pressed again and the liquid is collected in a fermenting vessel. It should be pale in colour;

browning indicates oxidation has taken place. During the soak it will have taken up a lot of flavour from the grape pomace and also a little sugar. Measure the gravity of the liquid which will be somewhere in the region of 10°0e. You should now chaptalise this up to 70°Oe so that the resulting country wine contains about 9% alcohol. The following table will give you the appropriate sugar addition.

**Chaptalisation table for pomace wine**

| Initial gravity (°Oe) | Amount of sugar to add to each gallon |
|---|---|
| 5 | 1lb 12oz (790g) |
| 10 | 1lb 11oz (760g) |
| 15 | 1lb 9oz (710g) |
| 20 | 1lb 6oz (620g) |
| 25 | 1lb 4oz (570g) |

After chaptalisation the procedure is precisely the same as for table wine described earlier. The finished product should be grapey and fresh. It will be light yet still posses a good flavour. It is ready to drink as soon as it is clear and should be finished within a year. It is a drink to enjoy when you feel you cannot justify opening a bottle of your best wine and it has one great advantage – being light it contains very few hangover-producing components and can be drunk greedily without ill effects!

# ℭ 17 Appreciation

I hope you will not think me presumptuous if I say a few words about appreciating your wine, but having taken the trouble to produce it every effort should be made to enjoy it!

One of the delights of growing your own wine is that it is possible to get the finest quality at less material expense than the cheapest country wine. Vines properly cared for will yield fine crops for a lifetime and apart from the occasional and quite insignificant cost of light chaptalisation, the juice needs no additional ingredient. It is little wonder that the vine is so affectionately regarded by man. Yet although your wine may cost you little, it should be drunk with as much care as has gone into its growing and vinting. Its temperature, the accompanying food, your surroundings and your mood will profoundly affect your enjoyment of a wine.

Probably more than 90% of the world's wine production is of everyday 'plonk'. To talk in hushed tones of its qualities would be pretentious nonsense. It is meant for quaffing without ceremony much as we drink tea. Yet even this ordinaire benefits from a little attention during serving – even to the point of exaggeration. A really rough red biddy will sometimes become quite palatable if it is warmed until it is near-tepid and a characterless and cloying Liberian Sauternes will be much improved by really good chilling!

Of course wine-serving rules can be taken to ridiculous extremes but most of them are established on common sense. Few people would enjoy a chilly red wine with Sole Bonne Femme, but tastes are quite individual and if such a choice really pleases you let no-one dissuade you. However the object of serving a wine at a certain temperature and in conjunction with certain food is to bring out is best qualities. A full-bodied red wine wine will not release its bouquet and flavour if it is cold. The volatile esters which affect the senses need warmth to vapourise them in order that they may be appreciated. Good red wines are usually best drunk when they are at about 18°C. White and rosé wines, on the other hand, show themselves off best when slightly chilled. They are frequently spoiled by over-chilling though and should not normally be served colder than 8°C. They should be fresh but not frigid or much of the flavour will be missed.

Often it is delightful to enjoy a wine of any sort just on its own. At other times wines go perfectly with certain dishes of food but some foods and flavours are the kiss of death to any wine. Very strong flavours such as curries will completely mask a wine. Vinegar in any noticeable

**Figure 32**   *Drinking glasses.*

quantity will make a wine taste like vinegar and it should be avoided like the plague. Strong citric flavours such as grapefruit, lemon or orange will have a similar if slightly less disastrous effect.

As to the best drinking glasses, let simplicity be your guide. Coloured bowls are an abomination for they will immediately deny you the pleasure of the wine's natural colour. I am not even very keen on coloured stems for they tint the wine confusingly. Some people go so far as to say that the bowl should be plain and uncut, but unless you are carrying out a *very* serious tasting I think this is being too fussy! A simple tulip or goblet glass will show off any wine to advantage. The one glass to avoid is that horrid article that used to be dragged out at weddings to hold warm champagne – it would be hard to conceive a less well-designed receptacle as it allows the rapid dissipation of the sparkle, which seems rather a pity after so much trouble has been taken to introduce it! Sparkling wines should be served in a tulip or flute, or even a silver goblet if you have one. but make sure it is very well washed after polishing unless you are partial to a *Silvo* bouquet.

Unless you are serving sparkling wine in a flute which may be almost topped up, fill your glass no more than half full. This will allow a space over the wine where the bouquet may collect and be appreciated. Note all the characteristics of the wine. Look at the colour, preferably with a white light or candle behind the bowl. If white, is it greenish, golden or almost crystal white, or if red is it purplish, brick-red or tawny? Is the bouquet clean or not? Is it flowery, fruity or complex? Is it rich and full or light and delicate, grapey or mature? Does the flavour complement the bouquet? Is it well balanced, soft or harsh, acid or dull, delicate or rich?

Do not be afraid to discuss your wine with other *interested* people – preferably other growers, but do not bore others. Be self-critical and listen to constructive criticism. Above all drink other people's wines and comparable commercial wines with your own sometimes or you will form a false impression of your own.

If all this sounds like a self-imposed end-of-term examination, it is in a way, but it should be a most enjoyable examination. Every year your wine will differ from the last. Each vintage is an exciting new experience and what in life can be more rewarding than that?

# Appendix A Suppliers

## Equipment

Amateur growers should be aware that many professional suppliers do not deal with very small orders. Those that supply *only* fully commercial growers are not included here. However, growers who are producing a few dozen bottles of wine can purchase much of what the need from the suppliers below, or from shops like the winemaking section of Boots the Chemists.

### *Vineyard Equipment*

**Secateurs (Felco)**
Your local gardening shop or Burton McCall, Samule Street, Leicester LE1 1RU

**Fungicides and herbicides**
Very small quantities are best obtained from your local gardening shop. Larger packs can be found at your nearest agricultural merchants.

**Plant guards (anti rabbit), post drivers, ground anchors, etc.**
J. Toms Ltd, Grigg Lane, Headcorn, Ashford, Kent TN27 9XT

**Twist-ties**
Gardening shops or GT Products, Accessories and Components, Chalk
Lane, Sidlesham, West Sussex PO20 7LW (Tel: 01243 641155)

**Refractometers**
Société Parisienne de Jumelles à Prismes, 9 Merivale Road, London
SW15 2NW

**Sprayers (knapsack and larger)**
GPS Sprayers, 3c Station Yard, Thame, Oxon OX9 3UH

## Vineyard sundries and harvesting equipment

Vigo Vineyard Supplies, Station Road, Hemyock, Devon EX15 3SE

## Cellar Equipment

Vigo Vineyard Supplies, Station Road, Hemyock, Devon EX15 3SE
A wide range of sundries and equipment for vinting and bottling comparatively small quantities, including grapemills and presses, yeasts,
reagents and test kits.

Rock Lodge Vineyard, Scaynes Hill, West Sussex RH17 7NG
Vinification reagents, finings, yeasts, etc.

## Filtration Equipment (for producers of reasonably large quantities)

Seitz Filtration (GB) Ltd., Bromyard Road Industrial Estate, Bromyard
Road, Ledbury, Herefordshire HR8 1LG

## Vines

These days, many garden centres stock a range of grapevine varieties,
and if you know of a local vineyard you may find they propagate vines

for sale as a side-line. The following suppliers will despatch vines by mail order:

Deacons Nursery, Godshill, Isle of Wight PO38 3HW

Highfield Nurseries, School Lane, Whitminster, Glos. GL2 7PL

Ken Muir, Honey Pot Farm, Weeley Heath, Clacton on Sea, Essex CO16 9BJ

Reads Nurseries, Hales Hall, Loddon, Norfolk NR14 6QW

Trevena Cross Nurseries, Breage, Helstone, Cornwall TR13 9PS

Vigo Vineyard Supplies (minimum quantity is 25 of any one variety), Station Road, Hemyock, Devon EX15 3SE

# Appendix B  Bibliography

Books that are out of print can usually be found through your local library.

Barrington Brock, R. *Viticulture Research Station Reports*, Jackmans Nurseries, Woking.

Barty-King, Hugh, *A Tradition of English Wine*, Oxford Illustrated Press.

Chancrin, W. and E. Long, *Viticulture Moderne*, Hachette.

Massel, A., *Basic Viticulture*, Heidleberg Publishers Ltd.

Massel, A. *Basic Oenology*, Heidelberg Publishers Ltd.

Moser, Dr Lenz, *The High Culture System*, Josef Faber Dounau, Austria.

Ordish, G., *Vineyards in England and Wales*, Faber, London.

Pearkes, Gillian, *Vinegrowing in the British Isles*, Dent, London.

Rook, W. A., *Diary of an English Vineyard*, Wine & Spirit Publications, London.

Smith, Jonna, *The New English Vineyard*, Sidgwick & Jackson.

Vogt, Prof., *Der Weinbau*, Ulmer Stuggart.

Winkler, A. J., *General Viticulture*, University of California Press.

# Appendix C  Conversion Tables

## *Imperial to metric*

| | |
|---|---|
| 1 fluid ounce (fl oz) | 28.4 millilitres (ml) |
| 1 pint (pt) | 568.3  millilitres (ml) |
| 1 gallon (gal) | 4.546 litres (l) |
| 1 ouce (oz) (avoirdupois) | 28.4 grams (g) |
| 1 pound (lb) (avoirdupois) | 453.6 grams (g) |
| 1 acre | 0.405 hectares (ha) |
| 1 foot (ft) | 0.3045 metres (m) |

## *Metric to Imperial*

| | |
|---|---|
| 1 litre (l) | 1.76 pints (pt) |
| 1 hectolitre (hl) | 22 gallons (gal) |
| 1 gram (g) | 0.035 ounces (oz) |
| 1 kilogram (kg) | 2.2 pounds (lb) |
| 1 hectare (ha) | 2.47 acres |
| 1 metre (m) | 3.28 feet (ft) |

## *Acid equivalents*

1g/l tartaric acid is equivalent to 0.653 g/l sulphuric acid
1g/l sulphuric acid is equivalent to 1.531 g/l tartaric acid

Appendix C: Cause and Effect

# Appendix D  Useful addresses

**United Kingdom Vineyards Association**
Church Road, Bruisyard, Saxmundum, Suffolk IP17 2EF
(Tel: 01728 638080).

Membership is open to commercial and *serious* amateur growers.

# ᴄꙅ Index